Unlocking Your Child's Potential is based on various workshops organized by Jan and Kateřina for children, students, and parents. I attended one of the workshops with my daughter Ema, and it was an extremely inspiring experience for both of us. It helped me discover my daughter's talents and made me believe that I had the power to help her get wherever she wants to be. Thank you, Jan and Kateřina!

— Terezie Tománková, TV presenter

Unlocking Your Child's Potential is a tremendous help for any parents who are concerned about their child's future in the modern world. I attended the Parent as a Positive Coach workshop organized by Jan and Kateřina when I was five months pregnant. I would like to use the principles they taught me to create the optimal conditions for my children to realize their potential in the future.

— Denisa Rosolová, former professional athlete and European champion

Jan and Kateřina have achieved something amazing. The book provides clear, concise guidelines for helping develop a child's talent and is a must-read for any parent. It offers numerous tips and suggestions that will help both you and your children live a better, fulfilled life.

— Radek Ptáček, clinical psychologist

I am extremely grateful that Jan and Kateřina joined forces to create this extremely helpful manual for parents. When you want to learn to cook, you buy a cookbook; when you want to learn to discover the best in your children and help them develop it, this is just the book for you. It teaches you that you should always try to do your best, but also that it's not the end of the world to make a mistake – every mistake is a valuable lesson. Both adults and children need someone who understands them and steers them in the right direction. I would like to thank Jan and Kateřina for sharing their experience with us. They set a path that everyone should follow.

— Veronika Kašáková, model and charitable foundation founder

There are myriad books on children and parenting, but the one you're reading has come just at the right time. We live in an age of great wealth and sometimes almost excessive hedonism, but also in an age that offers tremendous potential to those who know how to use it to grow and develop. And using it well is the key. We live in the golden age of humankind, trying to colonize space and discover distant galaxies, but more often than not, we don't really know ourselves. We are not aware of our own potential, skills, and abilities. This is where Jan and Kateřina come in, with their wealth of experience based on many years of collaboration. I hope the book will become an inspiration not only for parents and their children but for anyone who's interested in improving and understanding themselves.

— **Marian Jelínek, former personal trainer**
to Jaromír Jágr and currently a personal trainer
to Karolína Plíšková and other professional athletes

UNLOCKING YOUR CHILD'S POTENTIAL

UNLOCKING YOUR CHILD'S POTENTIAL: NURTURING BRILLIANCE & SHAPING FUTURES

JAN MÜHLFEIT & KATEŘINA KRŮTOVÁ

CAPSTONE
A Wiley Brand

Registered Office(s)
John Wiley & Sons Ltd, The Atrium, Southern Gate, Chichester, West Sussex, PO19 8SQ, UK
John Wiley & Sons, Inc., 111 River Street, Hoboken, NJ 07030, USA

For details of our global editorial offices, customer services, and more information about Wiley products visit us at www.wiley.com.

Wiley also publishes its books in a variety of electronic formats and by print-on-demand. Some content that appears in standard print versions of this book may not be available in other formats.

Library of Congress Cataloging-in-Publication Data is Available:

ISBN: 9781394239788 (Paperback)
ISBN: 9781394239801 (epdf)
ISBN: 9781394239795 (epub)

Cover Design: Wiley
Cover Image: © Dedraw Studio/Shutterstock; © TinyDoz/Shutterstock

SKY10064808_011324

TABLE OF CONTENTS

PART 3: BONUS INTERVIEWS

UNLOCKING YOUR CHILD'S POTENTIAL

0

INTRODUCTION

WHO WE ARE

Jan Mühlfeit and Kateřina Novotna organize workshops and lectures in both the Czech Republic and Slovakia, helping parents, students, and children unlock their human potential.

Jan: *Some 20 years ago, while I was still working for Microsoft, I first developed the concept of positive leadership. It's not about seeing everyone in a positive light – that would be impossible. Positive leadership means discovering a person's best qualities. Only then can you build teams where the whole is much more than the sum of its parts. It's a method suitable not only for corporate managers but also, for example, for sports coaches who want to create the world's best athletic teams. It allows you to mesh different personalities where one's strength can compensate for another's weakness. It's the combination of individual strengths, with a dash of inspiration, that makes a winning team – be it in sports, business, or art.*

Kateřina: *I've been working with children for over ten years. I find it incredibly fulfilling. A few years back, Jan and I had a sort of brainstorming session. In the end, we decided it would be great if we could join our two worlds and combine his long experience in personal development and positive leadership with my own focus on children, parents, and alternative methods of education. I believe through our workshops, lectures, and videos, as well as this book, we can share valuable information and experience with parents, children, and students, helping them follow their dreams and find an occupation they will enjoy and shine in. After all, we have done the same thing.*

Since we share the same goals, we have decided to write this book as a team and speak in plural for most of the time; sometimes, though, we might like to share some individual experiences, stories, or ideas, so we will add some comments as either Jan or Kateřina. As a bonus, we have added excerpts from an interview with our good friend and prominent Czech psychiatrist Cyril Höschl. (The complete interview with Cyril, as well as bonus interviews with Jaroslav Svěcený and Dagmar Svobodová, can be found at the end of the book).

WHY WE WROTE THIS BOOK

So far, about 1,400 children and 1,500 parents have attended our workshops, *Unlocking a Child's / Student's Potential* and *Parent as a Positive Coach*. We've made a very important observation: if parents understand themselves, they have a much better chance of understanding their children. You can't give what you don't have, as the old saying goes. Self-awareness gives parents the right tools to work with their child.

Few parents can claim to truly know themselves. Throughout our studies and careers, we learn to understand what's around us, not what's inside us. Many people will never get to explore their inner mental landscape and discover their strong points – things they are good at. They often end up doing a job they don't truly enjoy, and once they have children, they make them study things they have no aptitude for or that they don't really like, vicariously fulfilling their own ambitions through their offspring.

"People who study (insert a prestigious, lucrative field) can make good money," parents often argue, and send their children to study just such a subject. They might indeed end up making good money – but they will probably not be particularly happy. Once you manage to meet your basic needs, achieving true happiness requires a lot more than wealth (which you might already know, considering you are reading this book). That's why there are so many people in this world who are rich, successful – and very unhappy. Their only goal is to amass as great a fortune as possible, without having any true appreciation for their own work.

Our goal is to help both parents and children to discover their hidden talents, in order to live a better, fuller life and achieve contentment, success, and happiness. This is the purpose of both our workshops and this book, which discusses the concepts we teach in much greater detail. We would like this book to serve as a guide for parents who want more – both for their children and themselves.

OUR IDEAS AND APPROACH – AN OUTLINE

Parents wield an enormous influence over their children. Often, however, they don't realize how big that influence is, or they will not admit it to themselves. The way parents behave, the way they treat others, the way they talk about themselves and other people, their attitude toward work and leisure, their way of solving conflicts – in other words, virtually everything that parents do forms patterns that children soak up and model their own behavior on. Some of these patterns may not have an immediate effect but they imprint themselves on the child's subconscious. Years later, when the child has grown up, they may re-emerge and shape their personality and behavior.

At our workshops, we ask the parents the following questions:

How did you feel about your own growth and development when you were little, and how would you like to bring up your own children?

Most parents (about 90 percent) say that they don't want to repeat their parents' mistakes. They had decided, very early on, that they would never do such things to their children – and then they have children of their own, and they treat them exactly as their parents treated them. They are well aware that they have internalized some of the patterns of their childhood, but they have no idea how to break free from them.

Can you identify with this? You probably can. Don't worry – your brain has this amazing ability to reprogram itself. It's called neuroplasticity, and you will learn more about it in Chapter 1.

It's important to realize that you're doing something you don't want to do; only then can you change it.

PATIENCE IS AN IMPORTANT PART OF PARENTING

Most parents love their children unconditionally. Many are convinced that smoothing their children's path in life – explaining everything, buying them whatever they want, helping them out constantly – will make their children happier. More often than not, it doesn't work. Instead, try to be patient when your child is not as quick at mastering a task as their peers. Try not to step in when it takes them more time to learn things than you would have expected or if they don't master them right away. Be patient and support your children in learning things on their own. In doing so, you will help them far more than by doing everything for them. Overcoming obstacles builds up mental resilience – an ability to perform tasks even under stressful conditions. You won't learn anything if you stay in your comfort zone.

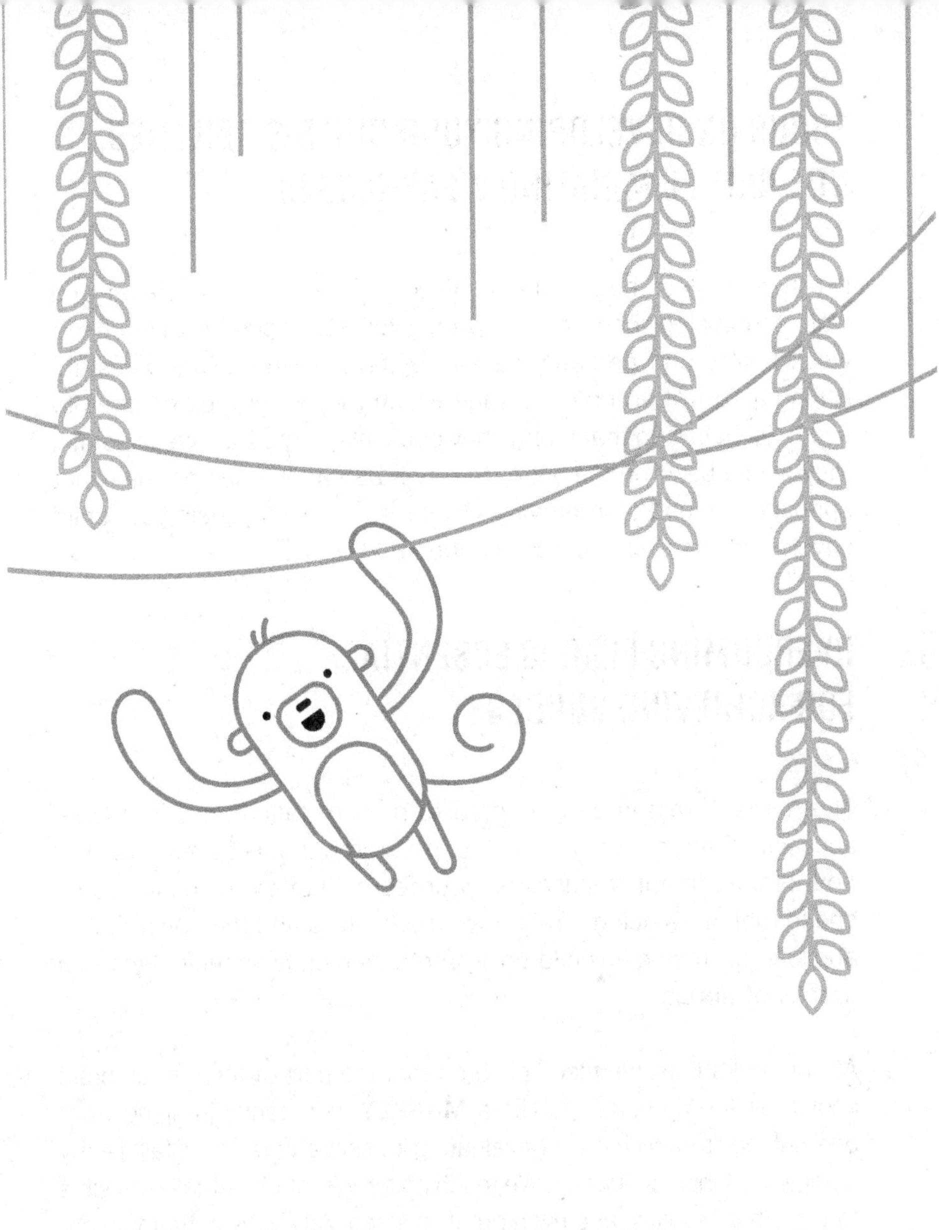

FOCUS ON DEVELOPING YOUR CHILD'S ABILITIES, NOT JUST ELIMINATING WEAKNESSES

It's important to help children discover their various talents and learn to develop them. Many parents tend to focus on their child's weak points and potential causes of failure. This leads to establishing a sort of arbitrary average which they want their children to aspire to, believing that if only they could eliminate their weak points, they would become the best. It's much better to focus on the exact opposite: instead of improving weaknesses, learn to help your child develop what they are actually good at.

OVERCOMING FEAR IS ESSENTIAL FOR ACHIEVING SUCCESS

The human brain is programmed to prevent failure, not to enable success. Overcoming this basic programming requires training. Your brain primarily focuses on your fears. That's why many people spend their lives being afraid – for themselves and their own future, and later for their own children. Parents then pass on their own fears to their offspring.

At our workshops, we teach children that the part of the human brain known as the amygdala is like a **MONKEY**, constantly jumping from one subject to another and evaluating possible causes of failure. By doing this, it incites our fear. We teach children that it's actually possible to tame the Monkey, and even put it to sleep. Any activity that you are good at and that you enjoy so much that you lose sense of time while doing it can calm down your inner Monkey. The total immersion in an activity, which leaves no room for fear and concerns, is also known as the flow state. (More about this in Chapter 1.)

The Monkey will accompany us throughout this book. Together, we will learn how to outsmart the Monkey, how to nourish it, and how to help children to become aware of their inner Monkey and get to know themselves better.

Join us! Stop living as a weak imitation and become an original instead!

This is not a perfect parent's handbook, but rather a friendly guide for anyone who would like to try out new methods of achieving better self-awareness and learn to communicate with their own children, helping them to lead a better, happier, more successful life.

A CHILD'S BRAIN IN THE EXPONENTIAL AGE

THE POWER OF BRAIN SYNAPSES

1

Every child is born with approximately 100 billion brain cells, called neurons. The neurons start interconnecting as early as during gestation. The links between neurons are known as synapses. Neurons interconnect depending on what the child sees, hears, and feels. The environment the child grows up in, the stimuli they receive, and what they play with are all crucial factors for forming brain synapses.

Bruce Lipton, prominent American developmental biologist and author of the book *The Biology of Belief*, claims that between the third trimester of gestation and seven years of age, a child lives in a kind of trance state, recording everything around them into their brain. Obviously, the better the software the child manages to "download" into their subconscious, the easier it will be for their personality to develop in a positive way in the future.

I'm sure you remember seeing your child so immersed in playing that they don't even hear you call them. How is that possible? How does a child become so absorbed in building with LEGO®, drawing, or putting together a jigsaw puzzle that they don't realize they're hungry or uncomfortable, or that someone is trying to talk to them? How come, whenever we become engrossed in an activity that we like and that we're good at, we don't take notice of time or anything going on around us? How can we focus on something to the point of not feeling thirsty or the need to use the bathroom?

In moments like this, we get into what is known as **flow** – a state of creative concentration which causes complete immersion in a game or activity. The condition was first described by Hungarian-American psychologist Mihalyi Csikszentmihalyi. In the 1980s and 1990s, Csikszentmihalyi observed various artists at work and noticed they sometimes became so absorbed with their activity that they forgot to eat, drink, or even sleep. Children have a natural ability to identify the activities that they have an aptitude for and prefer those activities to any others. They will not play with toys they don't like. Once a child becomes immersed in an activity they enjoy, they feel so energized that they quickly reach this flow state. Once in flow, they can't hear their parents calling, and even a toilet-trained child may sometimes wet themselves.

The concept of flow has been adopted by the field of positive psychology, and we will return to it many times throughout this book. It's very important to understand exactly how flow works and how to induce it consciously to achieve maximum motivation and produce the best possible results.

When we work in flow state, "work stops being work and turns into an experience, a supreme expression of our inner verve. (...) Furthermore, we are able to ignore all those annoying distractions that try to throw us off the ideal path toward our goal."[1]

We experience flow three times as often while working than during leisure time. This refutes the common concept of work as a necessary evil that allows us to make money and that we can only experience true happiness in our free moments. You cannot become creatively absorbed while watching TV or lying on a beach. Only when you engage in a task for which you have the required talent and skills, which is both a challenge and a productive use of your time, can you immerse yourself fully. Such tasks increase your self-confidence and your sense of happiness.

In flow state, two processes occur in your brain. The part of your brain known as the frontal cortex contains two important sensors:

- **Time perception sensor** – also known as our "**inner Watch**." Under usual circumstances, it perceives the passing of time very meticulously, but it shuts down when you reach flow state. A child has no sense of time passing, and they don't even hear their parents calling them.

For example, a child has been playing in the playground for over an hour. They're surprised and sad when their mother says it's time to go home. They feel like they couldn't have been playing for more than five minutes and don't want to go home just yet.

- **The amygdala** is a part of the brain associated with emotions. We've decided to call it **"the Monkey."** One of its tasks is to be on constant alert for any potential danger. The Monkey is one of the oldest parts of the human brain and performs a primary role in ensuring our survival. (In the past, it warned people against wild animals; today, it often acts up for no reason at all.) It is constantly active, jumping from one thing to another like a monkey between branches. However, once we reach flow state, it falls asleep and lets us explore and discover the world undisturbed.

Reading this book, you will get to know the Monkey much better. In Chapter 7, you will learn how to keep the Monkey happy and let both you and your child work and play in peace.

A child is building a complicated LEGO® structure, immersed in flow. They utilize their skills and abilities to the maximum to master this complex task. They sense nothing but the present moment; both the Watch and the Monkey are turned off. The child's parent comes by and looks at what the child has built. "I could never build anything that complex," they might think. "I've never even tried." The child has no such thoughts; they don't bother thinking about things they've built in the past or wonder whether the new project will work. They're only focused on placing the next brick just right. Their neurons form synapses with other neurons, ready and waiting to connect. This is how a child learns, while the parent concludes that, since they've never managed to build anything this complicated, they could probably never do it. Their Watch is running; their Monkey is jumping from branch to branch.

This is how everyone's brain works, whether you are an artist or athlete, adult or child.

Jan: *Olympic champion David Svoboda once told me at a coaching session that he had no memory of the final moments of his competition at the London Olympics. Only as he stood on the highest podium and listened to the national anthem did he realize he had actually won.*

There is one thing that is always with us in the "here and now," no matter what. It ensures our survival, and if it disappeared from the here and now, we would be dead: our breath. Breathing always happens in the present moment, and we can utilize it to calm down our inner Monkey. The inhale-exhale cycle takes approximately four seconds. Try it now. Breathe in and out.

And now, ask yourself the following question, and answer truthfully.

What were you thinking during that inhale-exhale moment?

The right answer is, of course, "Nothing."

When we perform a certain activity often enough, the synapses in our brain related to this particular activity become very strong, and a kind of sheath is formed around them, made of a substance called myelin. This process, known as myelination, allows nerve impulses to move far more quickly across the synapses and turns the activity at hand into a habit.[2] It becomes so ingrained and automated that you no longer have to think about it and can perform it even under difficult, stressful conditions. You work on autopilot, and your Monkey stays calm and dormant.

Some artists and athletes claim that it takes 10,000 hours of practice to become a master in their field.

~~~~~~~~~~~~~~~~~~~~~~~~~~~~~

Think about a child learning to play ice hockey. When they first put on the skates, they're just happy if they can stay upright. As they learn to skate, they focus on moving their feet and coordinating their movements on the ice. With practice, they get better and better. Once they're good enough to get a hockey stick, they no longer need to think about skating at all. Moving across the ice has become an ingrained, automated activity.

~~~~~~~~~~~~~~~~~~~~~~~~~~~~~

Once you turn an activity into an ingrained habit, you will be able to get in flow and perform even difficult, stressful tasks.

Imagine a child is working on his math test, immersed in a flow state. Then the teacher announces there are only ten minutes left to complete the test. At this point, there are two ways the child can react:

- They have enough practice doing their sums that the method has become ingrained (myelination has occurred). "I've already solved lots of such problems," they think. "Surely I can do two more in the time I have left." And they keep on working.

- The child becomes nervous and is no longer able to return to flow. The teacher's words throw them off. "Well, I've done some of the problems," they think, and keep on working, yet all the while being afraid they've made some mistakes, focusing excessively on not making any more. They focus their thoughts on the time they have left, afraid of failure.

This is how both adults and children react to various situations.

If a child has enough practice solving math problems, they are able to get into a flow state, even during a test, and stay in it until the last moment.

BRAINWAVES

Our brain is capable of operating on five brainwave frequencies. Each brainwave frequency correlates with a different state of consciousness. Just like sound frequencies, brainwave speed is measured in Hertz (Hz).

BRAINWAVES	FREQUENCY	ADULT PERSON'S STATE OF CONSCIOUSNESS
delta	0.5–4 Hz	deep sleep / unconsciousness
theta	4–8 Hz	light dream state / daydreaming / imagination
alpha	8–12 Hz	relaxed state of consciousness
beta	12–35 Hz	alert and focused state
gamma	over 35 Hz	peak concentration and performance

A child's brain operates on low brainwave frequencies – alpha and theta – which allows children to enter flow state very often. That's why children are so creative and imaginative.

Let's look at the theta brainwaves (4–8 Hz). The theta brain state is commonly associated with meditation or certain spiritual experiences. It is the state you experience just before drifting off to sleep, when various thoughts, images, and visions float across your mind. It is the dreamlike state when you are only half-awake but not yet in deep sleep. Theta brainwaves sometimes allow you to come up with great ideas or solutions to problems you haven't been able to find during the day. The theta brain state also occurs in REM sleep when you are dreaming.

Suggestion: Whenever you are simply resting or falling asleep, you may experience visions or come up with interesting ideas. Try to rouse yourself and write them down right away. Once you fall into a deeper sleep, you will have a hard time remembering them in the morning.

Kateřina: *When I lie in bed, just before I fall asleep, my body is completely relaxed, and thoughts just float around my head. That's when I tend to come up with the most interesting ideas. I try to make a quick note on my cell phone; if I forget to do that and fall asleep instead, I usually forget about them.*

The brains of preschoolers are in the theta state most of the time; that's why small children can be so creative and tend to become engrossed in a world of their own. They can easily imagine their toys coming alive. Toy animals can become real; a few twigs, pieces of bark, and moss can turn into a magical village where many fascinating stories can play out.

Suggestion: Try to recall such situations from your own childhood. Do you still remember what it was like, roaming around in a world of your own, where anything was possible? Can you recall the feeling of being so lost in your fantasies that you couldn't even hear your parents calling, forgot to turn up for lunch, or got unbelievably dirty while hiding in the shrubbery?

Memories like that are bound to put a smile on your face. Perhaps you will now realize that your children are not being naughty when they don't seem to listen to a word you say. Sometimes they become lost in their game at the most inconvenient moment. You are in a hurry, you don't want them to get dirty, or you are tired of repeating everything for the nth time. Remembering what you were like at their age may help you understand your child better and prevent you from getting needlessly angry.

Kateřina: *Sometimes, children can be too creative for their own good. I'm sure my mother vividly remembers the day I used wax crayons to draw on the wall, painted a picture above my bed using an apple cut in half, and used child safety scissors to cut leaves from all the plants I could reach. Her reaction was as far from the sandwich feedback (discussed in Chapter 5) as possible. However, not even her punishment could curb my boundless creativity. As parents, you don't have to feel guilty if you sometimes lose your temper. Children are quite resilient.*

A preschooler's mind is like a sponge: it absorbs everything it sees, hears, and senses and stores it in the subconscious. Most brain synapses are formed at preschool age: 50 percent form before the age of five, and by age seven your brain will have formed 75 percent of all the synapses it is capable of creating. They are all required for mastering the basic skills and abilities: learning to talk, read, write, and make sense of the world. During adolescence, some of the unused synapses start to disappear.

WINDOWS OF OPPORTUNITY

Windows of Opportunity are periods in a child's development during which they are able to master certain skills and concepts quickly and easily. Most Windows of Opportunity for specific areas of development occur until the age of six to seven.

If you want your child to speak a foreign language, it's best to start during the period when children are hard-wired for mastering speech and vocabulary, which is from birth until approximately six years of age. Most Windows of Opportunity come in preschool age; however, don't feel guilty for not exploring some of them fully. It doesn't mean that your child will never be able to master that specific skill, only that it will take a little more time or effort later on.

During each Window of Opportunity, it's important for parents to provide their child with as many stimuli and experiences as possible. Children also quickly absorb behavioral patterns they encounter in their own family, among their friends, or in nursery school.

Parents often argue or discuss "adult" problems in front of their children, believing that they are too small to understand what's going on. In fact, children take notice of everything happening around them and store it in their subconscious mind. Many years later, when they encounter similar situations, those long-stored patterns may come to light. Behavioral patterns often emerge only when a child grows up and starts a relationship or family.

It's quite normal for parents to lose their temper from time to time. We all make mistakes. It's important, however, to teach children that making mistakes is natural and that any problems can be resolved.

If you make a mistake, you can say: "I'm sorry I lost my temper. This is not how I wanted to behave." If your child behaves inappropriately, you can say: "I don't like it when you act this way. Let's talk about it."

Suggestion: As a parent, it's important to be honest. Don't pretend you can handle everything. If you let others help out, you're teaching your child an important lesson: you're showing them that you are not perfect and that you also need help from time to time. Show your child that different people have different talents and that it's great to work as a team where everyone has something to contribute. Your child will absorb these patterns and learn to function within a family.

You don't need to feel guilty about having neglected an important aspect of your child's development. Nobody is perfect. Instead, try to realize where you went wrong and consciously improve your attitude whenever a similar situation occurs. In doing so, you will be giving your child plenty of material to store in their subconscious.

There is usually more than one way to handle a certain problem. Try to realize that you can do things differently than you are used to doing them, and you don't have to follow your parents' example. Don't be afraid to try your own way.

HELPING YOUR CHILD BUILD BRAIN SYNAPSES

There are various ways you can help your child create brain synapses. They include various simple or complex memory games, rhythmic exercises (clapping out a beat, making sounds using your own body), and activities stimulating motor development (turning around, walking along a line, playing with modeling clay, stringing beads). You have most likely tried out many such activities with your child. Children see them as a fun game, but, at the same time, they're helping your child develop and improve.

Here are some simple exercises you can try with your child to develop specific parts of their brain.

SPATIAL PERCEPTION

Twirling around helps children develop spatial perception. You can start with simple exercises as early as age three. First make the child twirl following one hand, then the other, or following various pictures. Walking along a line is another good exercise to improve spatial perception. Stretch a length of string or a jump rope on the floor and let the child walk on it. This is a very good balance exercise. Both exercises help the child develop a sense of space – even when they fall down.

Brain Gym® is a method using various exercises to improve hand, foot, and eye coordination, as well as the mind, which controls our movement.[3]

EXERCISE: BRAIN GYM®

Here are some simple exercises both you and your children can try:

- Draw number eights with your finger or your entire arm (you can try moving your other hand in the opposite direction).

- Use your finger to draw various figures in the air (letters, simple images).

- Take slow, long sips of water, and try to sense the water running through your body.

- Alternate regular and irregular breathing, and try to feel the changes, or try belly breathing.

> • Try to conduct a verbal and non-verbal activity simultaneously: do one of the previous exercises while talking, or try to draw or write while talking, in order to improve your attention.

ENGAGING THE SENSES

Children retain new things much better if learning them engages all their senses. This approach is applied in the Montessori Method of Education (see Chapter 2). Its founder, Maria Montessori, followed the principle of "learning by doing," somewhat similar to the teachings of Czech theologian and educator John Amos Comenius.

Whenever possible, children should learn by touching, feeling, hearing, or seeing things in their natural environment. This is especially beneficial for building new brain synapses.

EXERCISE: RECOGNIZING FLAGS

Teaching your child to recognize national flags can involve a number of small visual activities: learning and identifying colors, describing various symbols and ornaments, and so on. You can also talk about the different countries the flags belong to: what kind of people live there, what they like to eat... Perhaps you could even try making some of their national dishes! You can play the countries' national anthems or folk songs and learn a few phrases in their language. This will help your child engage as many senses as possible, and it supports the development of associative thinking. This is especially important during preschool age when synapse building is at its peak.

Kateřina: *When I used to babysit children, I always tried to spend as much time outside with them as I could. One of our favorite games was "potion making." We picked various leaves, flowers, and plants, sniffed* *everything, and then mixed it with dirt, pebbles, or even cooking ingredients (which we could actually taste). Then we mixed it all with water. Every potion was unique, and we would try to make up interesting names for them. Children tend to enjoy playing with water, and simple activities like this one can involve all their senses: touch, smell, taste, sight, and hearing. Children can also improve their imagination by making up various stories about the potions and their magical effects.*

CONCENTRATION AND FOCUS

In a world full of modern technologies, it's hard to maintain our concentration and focus on a single thing. Developing concentration in children is even harder. PlayWisely® is a developmental play system which supports a child's natural learning and movement ability, engaging all the senses and improving concentration. It is a set of fun activities for both children and parents. PlayWisely® is a comprehensive, scientifically proven method of learning by play, which uses each child's natural ability to learn and move, from birth to preschool age.

PlayWisely® was founded by Patty Hannan, former American gymnast and neuroscience specialist. The system uses **sensory activities**, which help develop a child's concentration, memory, and language skills, and **motor exercises**, which improve a child's mobility, agility, and motor skills.

PlayWisely® uses a set of special flashcards that show various images, words, numbers, colors, and objects of different sizes and shapes. Used jointly with the directional orientation method, the flashcards offer a unique set of activities that allow children to experience the fun of moving, learning, and discovering. A typical PlayWisely® class lasts 30–45 minutes, depending on the child's age, and is divided into several activity blocks. Children start playing with flashcards, followed by mobility exercises, and ending with another set of flashcards.[4]

EXERCISES BASED ON THE PLAYWISELY® METHOD

You can either buy the original PlayWisely® flashcards or create a set of your own.

Sit directly facing your child and show them the flashcards in quick succession. The cards should have a simple image – an apple, for example – but the apple's shape, size, and position should change on each card. It can be on the top or bottom, left or right, hidden behind something, be smaller or bigger, have a different color, and so on. Show card after card to your child and add a quick comment on each one ("apple on top, apple on the bottom, apple behind a tree, green apple, red apple..."). Older children can describe the cards themselves as the parent flashes them.

PlayWisely® is offered by licensed centers and in some nursery schools and kindergartens. To better understand the PlayWisely® method, you can watch various videos on YouTube showing the flashcard system and other exercises.

ASSOCIATIVE THINKING

Most standard schools are not particularly big on developing associative thinking. Subjects are taught separately – a math lesson is followed by a lesson devoted exclusively to reading or writing. This method does not support learning through associations, in which a child puts together information based on their connection to real life.

EXERCISE: MEMORY TRAINING

As a memory training exercise, learn various synonyms for any new words you pick up in either a foreign language or your native language (for example, for "beautiful" you could also learn "nice," "pretty," etc.), or associate a particular thing with that word (story, experience, emotion; if we use "beautiful" again, imagine something you consider beautiful). When you're performing under pressure and can't recall a certain word, knowing three synonyms for that word, or remembering a place or emotion connected with it, will make recalling the word and its context much easier. If you only memorize the word itself, you might not be able to remember it under stress at all.

EXERCISE: ENIGMATIC RIDDLES

Enigmatic riddles are logical puzzles hidden in a story. They improve children's focus and attention span (by having to understand the instructions and reading the story), as well as creativity and associative thinking. Based on the information provided within a story, a child has to make the right connections in their brain and find a logical solution. Such riddles may seem difficult at first sight (number sequences especially); however, the harder the problem, the more overjoyed your child will be once they solve it.

Even a seemingly unsolvable riddle looks easy once someone gives you a hint or tells you the solution. "How could I have not seen it?" you think.

Story for small children: It's a beautiful spring day. Grandma has taken her grandchildren for a walk in the woods around her little cottage. They went around a rotten tree stump, stumbled over a hedgehog, and saw a couple of roe deer. At the edge of the forest, they found a small heap of coals, a pot, and a carrot.

What do you think happened there?

Solution: Let the children come up with various possible solutions – someone might have built a snowman during the winter; someone has been camping there and made soup over the open fire, and so on. You can be as creative as you want and create your own stories.

Logical sequences are collections of numbers or other objects that follow a particular logical pattern. Sequences can be made up of numbers, letters, or pictures.

Exercise for older children and students – Present your child with the following sequence of letters:

T T T ? F S S ? N H

Encourage the child to find the logical pattern in the sequence and add the missing letters.

If the child is stuck, you can give them a hint by adding the missing letters:

T T T F F S S E N H

Don't tell them what the pattern is; let them try and find out. You could give them a hint by telling them that the letters are somehow connected with numbers – perhaps they could start counting out loud?

Some logical sequences may be difficult even for parents to solve. Take your time and don't rush finding the solution. Put up the sequence somewhere you can see it (on the fridge, for example) and try thinking about it from time to time.

Solution: The sequence is made up of the first letters of the numerical sequence from ten to one hundred, counting by tens (ten, twenty, thirty, etc.).

Exercise for older children and students: You can either write this sequence in a column or in a row, depending on what you find easier.

1
11
21
1211
111221   1 11 21 1211 111221 312211 ????????
312211
????????

Solution: Each subsequent line repeats and describes the numbers on the previous line.

1
11 (one number one – 1× 1)
21 (two number ones – 2× 1)
1211 (one number two and one number one – 1× 2 and 1× 1)

29

ABSTRACT PERCEPTION

Children are naturally inquisitive and are always on the lookout for new things to learn or discover. Offer them opportunities to do this from an early age.

Recognizing various symbols, images, or patterns is a great exercise. Children like learning and remembering things adults often find useless: car license plates, timetables, or subway stops. Children love discovering new things around them and tend to memorize even the most nonsensical things.

Kateřina: *As a child, I often got bored while bathing. I entertained myself by memorizing various instructions and ingredient lists on the shampoo and soap bottles, even if they were in a foreign language. I didn't understand most of it and couldn't read some of the letters, so I simply skipped them, making up my own silly "shampoo sentences." I can still remember some of them today.*

EXERCISE: COGWHEELS

When you spin all the cogwheels, in which direction is the last wheel going to turn?

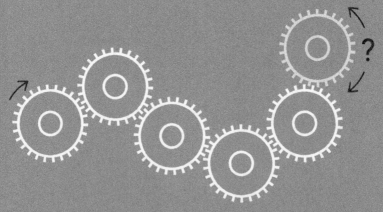

THE POWER OF BRAIN SYNAPSES

Show the children various options to find the correct answer. Some children think visually, turning the cogwheels in their head; others will use their finger to "turn" the wheels. Some children might actually realize that each odd and even wheel is going to spin in the same direction and then count out the result (using a mathematical approach).

Solution: The last wheel is going to spin left (counterclockwise).

Let the child find their own way to reach a solution. Only then can you show them other possible methods. Then show them another picture with an even longer cogwheel chain. Will they use the method they discovered on their own or try another way?

Most children are naturally inquisitive. If you give them several options, hinting at a possibly easier solution, they will want to try it out for themselves.

Solution: The last wheel is going to spin left (counterclockwise).

EXERCISE: TRIANGLES

What is the last triangle going to look like?

Solution: The arrow is going to point down and to the left, toward the grey line. Again, there are several possible ways to solve this problem. You can either do it by color, since the arrow always points to the grey line, or you can follow the directions of the arrows and find out which direction is missing.

You can also sort the diagram into pairs and then look for connections. The two top left triangles are exact opposites, just like the two bottom left triangles, which means that the last two triangles are also going to be exact opposites.

Which approach did you use? Did you focus on colors, shapes, or pairs? Try to use the method that feels the most natural to you. Similarly, let your children use the method they find easiest. Finding out what our brain tends to focus on and the best way we learn can help us study and think better.

NTC Learning is a program to promote motor and cognitive abilities in children, based on the principles of associative thinking and identifying abstract symbols. Designed by Serbian physician and psychologist Ranko Rajović, it combines the development of analytical thinking with motor exercises, such as spinning around or balance exercises. The program supports the engagement of all senses, for example, through listening to music.

CREATIVITY ON THE DECLINE

A survey conducted by NASA found that 98 percent of children at the age of six show extremely high creativity. This is because we give them a lot of opportunities to play and discover the world on their own terms.

But what happens afterwards, in most of the world?

They go to school.

At age ten, only 30 percent of children are still highly creative; a mere 15 percent stay creative at age 15; and only 2 percent retain high creativity even after they graduate college and look for a job. Compared to age six, the percentage has reversed exactly: 98 percent of children who have a happy childhood in a good family are highly creative at preschool age; once they pass through the education system, only 2 percent remain creative by age 25. Does this mean that school systematically and gradually suppresses children's creativity?

One of the possible reasons could be that at school, children are not allowed to explore and examine things. One of the fundamental questions which stimulates human progress is this:

Is there another way of doing that?

This question stimulates human beings' natural inquisitiveness. We would still be living in caves if people throughout history didn't ask themselves whether there could be a better way of doing things. This usually led to a creative idea, resulting in an important invention or innovation. The sooner a child learns that it is natural and beneficial to ask this question, the sooner they will discover their own talents and strengths – and the lower the chance that the school system will repress their natural desire to learn and move forward.

~~~~~~~~~~~~~~~~~~~~~~~~~~~~~~~~~~~~~~~

In a math class, Joe asks the teacher: "Is there another way to solve this problem?"

"Sit down, Joe," the teacher says. "Mary will now repeat to us the only possible method. That is what's in your textbooks, and that's how we're going to do it."

~~~~~~~~~~~~~~~~~~~~~~~~~~~~~~~~~~~~~~~

Joe will probably never ask again. The teacher's attitude allows no space for creativity, and it's a sure-fire way to kill a child's natural inquisitiveness.

Over the past 300 years, the school system has not changed much. Despite the fact that there are many wonderful teachers with a natural talent for working with children and who highly enjoy their job, the traditional education system does not allow them to support each child's uniqueness. Most contemporary school systems encourage conformity so that all children are more or less on the same level, creating a sort of artificial average.

Jan: *Back when I was still in school, we were taught that brain cells start dying off around age 30. Thankfully, it was later discovered that this is not true, thanks to the ability of the brain known as neuroplasticity.*

Neuroplasticity is the brain's ability to change throughout a person's life. Many aspects of the brain are "plastic," which means that, with enough persistence, it can be altered or reprogrammed, even later in life. Do not despair if you feel like your child's school does not allow them to develop as much as they could, or that you have not done enough for your child's mental growth, and now you can't do anything about it. It's never too late. Even an adult can reprogram their brain. If you discover a certain talent or ability later in life, even in old age, you can consciously start to explore and improve it, which will slowly but surely alter your brain. It will just take longer than it would have taken you early in life. A small child can easily learn three foreign languages, often almost simultaneously; if you wanted to do the same thing at age 25, it would be much harder, and it would be even more difficult at age 50 – but not impossible. Research using computed tomography has discovered that the method of building new brain synapses is the same in children and adults – the only difference is the speed of them re-forming, which declines with age. Remember the Windows of Opportunity we talked about earlier? That's exactly what it's about.

HOW TO DEVELOP CREATIVITY IN CHILDREN

Jan: *In my radio talk-show,* Thinking First League, *Czech actor Ondřej Brzobohatý once told me that his father used to tell him and his sister stories before bedtime. The children could make up what the story would be about, and they could decide the ending. This simple evening ritual was a great way to develop their creativity and imagination.*

Here are a few exercises you can try with your children to support and develop their creativity.

EXERCISE: STORIES WITH PREDETERMINED WORDS

During afternoon rest or before bedtime, make up simple stories with your child. First ask your child to come up with three to five words that must appear in the story. Based on those words, create a simple story (or even a long, complicated one) and tell it to your child. By making up the words, the child has the power to influence the story, which is something children enjoy.

Once your child has mastered the storytelling game, you can reverse roles. You will be the one making up words, and your child will tell the story (with your help if needed).

EXERCISE: THROW THE DIE, DESIGN A VEHICLE[5]

This game can be played in a group or with a single child. You will need a die, a pencil or crayons, and several sheets of paper.

ENVIRONMENT	TYPE OF PROPULSION	PURPOSE
1. air	1. gasoline	1. sport
2. water	2. nuclear power	2. military
3. ground	3. methane	3. exploration
4. space	4. jet propulsion	4. passenger transport
5. mountains	5. horse-drawn	5. romantic
6. underwater	6. steam power	6. animal transport

Copy this table onto a sheet of paper for everyone to see. Each throw of the die determines one of the vehicle's properties. Each player rolls the die to determine the type of environment their vehicle will travel in. Once all the players have rolled, they start a second round to decide how the vehicle will be powered. The third roll determines the vehicle's purpose. Once all the players have rolled the die three times, they can start designing their vehicle. You can either have everyone draw their vehicle and show it to the others or just tell everyone about it.

Kateřina: *My brother is three and a half years older than I am. He's always been my partner in crime and a great role model. He used to take me everywhere with him. I copied everything he did and learned so much from him. Naturally, we fought a lot, but he was great at making up creative and fun games for me. One of them, "What kind of silence?"*

is actually a great tip for parents who need their children to calm down and rest, and develop their creativity and imagination at the same time.

My brother made up this game for me when I was still a preschooler. We shared a room, and I used to talk his ear off before bedtime. He invented an amazingly creative way of shutting me up.

GAME: WHAT KIND OF SILENCE?

You can either try out this game right before bedtime or before the afternoon nap. Pretend you have become a host of an amazing television contest and your child is the contestant, or one of several contestants. (My brother would often change voices to imitate other contestants, which sometimes included famous people.)

The game has two rounds.

Round 1: The host/parent asks: "What kind of silence are we going to have?"

Now it's up to the contestant to make up a name for their silence – as creative and original as possible: gray-brown silence, clay silence, flying unicorn silence, grandpa's old sock silence, and so on.

The host/parent then starts a countdown: "3... 2... 1... go!" For at least five seconds, the child has to stay absolutely quiet, to show everyone how marvelous their silence "sounds."

Round 2: The host/parent continues: "Well done! What an amazing silence that was! You've made the grand finale!"

Obviously, the grand finale is complete silence for the whole night.

You can spice up the game by conducting a short interview with the contestant/child to help them get into their part and look forward to the grand finale, when they can show everyone that their silence is the absolute best.

Suggestion: Children can sometimes play alone. They're perfectly able to make up fabulous games on the spot and develop their creativity all on their own. There's no need to set up a detailed play schedule and entertain your child for every minute of their day.

SCHOOL VS. INNOVATION

2

WHAT TRADITIONAL SCHOOLING IS ABOUT

The standard school system, as we know and remember it, encourages **individualism**. Students and pupils listen, study, and present what they have memorized, and they are evaluated based on their ability to do this. Individual testing is obviously important, but once the children grow up and enter the professional world, either as employees or freelance specialists, they will soon realize that what is truly important is teamwork. Every professional endeavor is a team effort, and cooperation within a team is an important skill – which is, unfortunately, rarely taught in school. Even higher education institutions (high schools, colleges, and universities) hardly ever include classes that require teamwork – perhaps with the exception of various chemical and biological lab seminars, where students are divided into groups and assigned various experiments (albeit more motivated by the limited amount of lab equipment than an actual desire to teach teamwork).

When children actually try to cooperate, it's called copying or plagiarizing, and the culprits involved usually get a failing grade.

Jan: *I used to lead teams of thousands of people. Those who were good team players were appropriately rewarded.*

- School tends to divide the curriculum into **separate subjects**. This is undeniably important, but it's equally important to be able to connect various pertinent information from the specialized subjects.

Healthcare and medical specialists are becoming increasingly aware that it is necessary to treat the human being as a whole, instead of only addressing the specific body part or organ in trouble. "The biomedical model views a human being as a sort of a live biological machine

41

with certain parts malfunctioning," says prominent Czech psychiatrist Radkin Honzák. "Feelings and emotions play no part in this. Medical professionals have no idea how sadness (and I mean actual sadness, not clinical depression) or joy affect the human body. Emotions are a function of the body, but ever since Plato, they have been treated as coming from the soul – which means they have no place in medicine. However, patients who are cheerful and optimistic react to treatment quite differently than sad or anxious patients."[6]

- School **punishes children for making mistakes**. Making mistakes in a test means a worse grade, followed by parental reproach. Some schools are particularly strict in grading tests, and even one minor mistake can lower the child's grade. However, without making mistakes we would never improve and move forward. Mistakes and errors are virtually demonized in the current school system. It would be far better to treat mistakes as transformative moments. If a child makes a mistake but receives no public shaming for it, they are far more likely to remember where they went wrong and try to find another way of solving the particular problem.

There's one important thing both adults and children should remember: **Mistakes are something that's already happened**. They're in the past and you cannot change them. The only thing you *can* do is learn from them. Instead of rehashing the past, find out where you went wrong, and go back to the present. The present moment is the only thing we have, and the present also means a gift – one that we have all been given – and it's up to us how we use it. When we make a mistake, we often keep going over it constantly. "I made a mistake on this test (in the game). One mistake. I'm definitely going to blow the whole test (lose the game) now." Our Monkey is frantic, jumping around like a maniac, and won't let us concentrate and focus back on the present moment.

Jan: *Bill Gates used to tell me: "If you're not sure whether you should do something, just do it. You can always ask for forgiveness later." And there were times where I did indeed have to ask for forgiveness. If you approach your mistakes the same way, they will become a bridge that will lead you toward better results in the future. Think about it and try it out.*

Obviously, it's not a good thing to repeat the same mistakes over and over again.

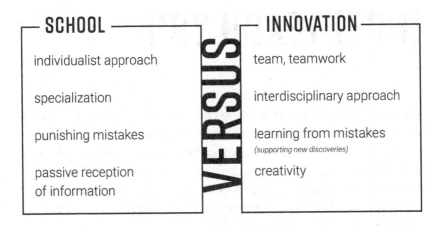

SCHOOL	VERSUS	INNOVATION
individualist approach		team, teamwork
specialization		interdisciplinary approach
punishing mistakes		learning from mistakes *(supporting new discoveries)*
passive reception of information		creativity

Traditional school uses the principle of **passive learning**. Children are required to memorize information and opinions that they are not allowed to question and then regurgitate the knowledge on a test. Once they enter the professional world, however, they will need to search for possible solutions, cooperate, think creatively, and come up with innovations. The ability to innovate depends on our level of creativity. Now you probably understand why children rapidly lose their creative potential once they start school. Traditional schools are not particularly big on teaching children cooperation or developing creativity. Passive learning does not take advantage of the flow state and its benefits in the learning process.

WHAT SCHOOL WILL (NOT) TEACH YOU

Traditional school focuses on things that are all *around* us. It teaches children to read and write, do sums, and acquire information. This is certainly crucial for children's learning, development, and overall intellectual growth. However, the emphasis on memorizing and dividing the curriculum into separate subjects does not support true immersion in the subject and does not encourage creativity based on a child's particular interests. An interdisciplinary approach is a little more common at high school and college levels.

Unfortunately, however, traditional school does not work with what is *inside* us. It does not allow children to explore the inner workings of their mind. Knowing how your brain works could save you hours of studying, both in school and at home. Learning to understand your own values and priorities will help you function better in all aspects of your life and will allow you to stand your ground and defend your opinion, even under pressure. Once you have a clear idea of who you are – and why you are who you are – you will be free to ponder your mission in life and its meaning. Teaching children to understand and handle their emotions at elementary school level could save them many a personal failure and disappointment later in life.

Self-awareness is a key skill that helps you deal with the demands and challenges of life. Unfortunately, it is not a skill that is taught in elementary school. Children memorize what is around them but have no idea what is inside them.

As parents, you can help children discover their inner world. This will help them improve their self-awareness and grow into a well-rounded adult.

What they will (not) teach you in school:

WILL	WILL NOT
English	How your brain works
Mathematics	Your values
History	Thoughts & memories
Physics	Self-image
Biology	Emotions
Other subjects	Identity
→ a.k.a. What's around us	→ a.k.a. What's inside us

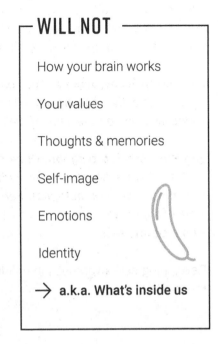

Jan: *When I first started promoting the concept of positive leadership, I was invited to give three lectures at Harvard University and one at MIT. Over 600 students turned out. Those two schools are considered to be the best in the world. They routinely produce CEOs of major companies, successful politicians, and other prominent people. During each lecture, I asked the students whether they had ever attended a self-awareness course. Out of those 600, only 11 raised their hands. Even the best schools in the world will not teach you self-awareness.*

Remember the pre-flight safety instructions delivered by a flight attendant before your plane takes off? They always tell you what to do in case of decompression: fit your own oxygen mask before helping children or anyone else requiring assistance. Self-awareness is just like that. To be able to understand and help people, you first need to understand yourself. To help their child grow up and mature, parents should first understand themselves and be aware of their own life goals.

If you are not self-aware enough, you may occasionally be able to get into flow state, but you will not be able to maintain it for a prolonged period. Those who have conscious control over their flow state can become the true masters in their field.

Jaroslav Svěcený, violinist: *I can only get in flow once I have mastered a piece perfectly. I no longer need to concentrate on playing; my hands suddenly seem to have a life of their own.*

Jan Pirk, cardiac surgeon: *Once I get in the operating room, I can work for several hours in a row without being aware that I'm actually operating. I work on autopilot. Early in my career, I realized that the work of a cardiac surgeon was sort of like being a plumber combined with a seamstress.*

Developing self-awareness in children will be discussed in Part 2 of this book.

PROGRESSIVE EDUCATIONAL METHODS

According to research conducted by the McKinsey consulting company, achieving flow state improves performance by 500 percent, creativity by 400 percent, and speed of learning by 450 percent, compared to people unable to get in flow. That is why some progressive schools and educational methods take advantage of the benefits of flow in teaching children.

As authors of this book, we particularly value the Montessori Educational Method, John Amos Comenius' concept of "school by play," and certain traits of the Waldorf education movement. We will now discuss these in more detail.

MONTESSORI EDUCATIONAL METHOD

The Montessori Educational Method was developed in the early 20th century by Italian physician Maria Montessori. The motto of Montessori education is "help me to do it myself." The teacher is not a figure of authority but rather a guide helping the child explore various options and work independently. Montessori's "learning by doing" concept, which emphasizes learning through practical experience, is loosely based on the teachings of John Amos Comenius.

A Montessori lesson lasts 90 minutes instead of the usual 45. The standard 45-minute class is too short for children to achieve flow, immerse themselves in an activity, and work without constant interruptions. Standard-length classes force children to interrupt their workflow too soon, and after a short break they are forced to focus on a different subject altogether. Why interrupt their concentration and euphoric state if they could easily stay in flow much longer?

In a Montessori school, a child can spend the entire 90-minute lesson studying a mathematical problem they are interested in. They can get fully immersed in their work, and getting into flow helps them master the subject faster and more effectively. The Montessori system does not require that all children in a class be on the same level. Some seven year olds may be able to solve complex math problems using four-digit numbers; others may not yet have gotten beyond doing sums up to 20. Montessori elementary schools have mixed-age groups (6- to 9-year-olds, 9- to 12-year-olds, 12- to 15-year-olds), where the older children help the younger ones, and the younger ones can often be more advanced than their older classmates. This prevents unhealthy competition among children.

Kateřina: *That's one of the things I really like about the Montessori system. Why should all seven-year-old children be on the same level in reading, writing, and math? What if a child learns to read at age four and sits bored in a class where the others are still learning their first letters? What if another child has trouble reading even in second or third grade and feels stupid compared to their classmates? In the traditional school system, a child's intellect and skills are measured by the grades they receive, which leads to some children feeling "better" or "worse" than others. I think that mixed-age groups give children an opportunity to develop at their own pace in various subjects. People sometimes object that the oldest children within each age group are hampered in their progress by the younger children. In fact, the opposite is true. Children have the chance to explain their newly acquired knowledge to their younger classmates, which helps them master and retain the information much more effectively. Montessori classes encourage cooperation and helping others. The smallest children can learn by observing and imitating their older schoolmates. As children progress to higher age groups, they get to be both the youngest ones and the experienced old hands, which in turn boosts their self-confidence or allows them to revise their knowledge along with the younger children.*

Children enjoy utilizing their talents and skills to learn. The Montessori system allows children to pick whatever learning aids and materials they find easiest to master each subject. Each child may prefer to use different materials, depending on their particular talents. Choosing a particular learning aid determines the way the child has chosen to master the particular subject. Visually oriented children, for example, may learn math differently than logical thinkers.

Jan: *I am somewhere in the middle of the visual and logical approach, which means I am a little bit of both.*

Children who attend Montessori schools tend to achieve better results than children from traditional schools, probably because they are in a better learning environment.

The term "Montessori mafia" was first coined in a 2011 *Wall Street Journal* article. It refers to the fact that a number of prominent corporate leaders and CEOs attended Montessori schools, which has given them the skills required to steer their companies toward innovations and succeed on the global market.

WALDORF EDUCATION

Schools based on the Waldorf system of education now number thousands all over the world.

Waldorf education is based on the educational philosophy of Rudolf Steiner, Austrian philosopher and the founder of Anthroposophy. Unlike traditional schools, which almost exclusively focus on developing the students' intellect and memorizing information, Waldorf pedagogy views a human being as an integral part of nature and its laws, striving to develop pupils' intellectual, artistic, and practical skills in an integrated and holistic manner. It emphasizes the cyclical nature of life and the importance of rituals and customs. It encourages students to work with natural materials and supports artistic imagination and creativity.

The Waldorf system greatly emphasizes cooperation and team spirit. Students do not have standard textbooks but make their own (sometimes with their parents' help). Waldorf schools start teaching foreign languages from an early age. Children often start learning two foreign languages in the first grade, which is common in international schools but very rare in the traditional school system.

Just like Montessori schools, the Waldorf system does not use the traditional grading system but instead uses written assessment. Assessment is commonly used in many progressive education systems; traditional schools are not too keen on it, unfortunately.

Kateřina: *Some parents might object that progressive education methods are not suitable for every child. Some children require a strict routine and guidance and are happier with the standard grading system, parents often claim. All of these objections have a clear answer: progressive methods are suitable for virtually every child, but they are not for every parent. Parents who decide on a particular method of education for their child should be in agreement with the school's methods, and their lifestyle and family values should loosely reflect this. Parents with an authoritative approach to raising children tend to compare their child's achievements with other children and require that their child receives a clear-cut evaluation. Placing such a child in a school using progressive methods would only make the child insecure, both in school and at home.*

COMENIUS' "SCHOOL BY PLAY"

John Amos Comenius was a 17th-century Czech philosopher, theologian, and educator, whose works laid the foundations of modern education. In 1630, Comenius published *Schola Ludus* ("School as a Game") – a collection of eight plays which were supposed to improve students' knowledge of Latin. In dramatic form, he presented students with basic knowledge in all the major fields of the time, as well as his own ideas on the stages and methods of education. Comenius claimed that simply lecturing the children about a certain topic will not help them retain the knowledge, because they are only using one of the senses during learning. Showing and telling, which engages two senses, significantly improves knowledge retention. Active involvement in the learning process, during which children use several senses at once, turns the acquired knowledge into a usable skill.

Comenius' method is similar to learning in the flow state. A child learning in flow enjoys what they're doing, since they're utilizing their best skills to achieve the result. This creates an emotional connection to the subject at hand and helps children retain and utilize the knowledge in the long term. Once the knowledge a child is trying to learn turns into a skill (habit), the synapses built in the process will remain in place for the rest of their life. Unfortunately, the traditional Czech schooling system incorporates only a scant few of Comenius' tenets. Standard schools encourage mediocrity and herd mentality. The emphasis on memorizing kills the students' natural inquisitiveness and hinders their development. Innovations require a stress-free environment and conditions that we have described previously. Children should focus on the subjects they are good at so that they can develop their talent and achieve success,[7] not strive to improve in subjects they have no aptitude for. Obviously, children need to learn even those subjects they are not particularly good at to complete a well-rounded education; however, educators should not overlook the child's strengths in order to improve their weaknesses.

Such an approach results in the child constantly trying to catch up with the classmates who have a natural aptitude for a particular subject. Often, they're only doing it to make their parents happy and avoid being compared unfavorably to their friends ("How come Philip can do this and you can't?" "Look what nice handwriting Anne has!" "All of your classmates can do it; I don't see why you shouldn't be able to!").

This leads to the child comparing themselves with others and never being satisfied with their effort.

Jan: *Scholars and educators often criticize me for not addressing people's weaknesses. I realize people have their weak points which they need to improve so they won't hinder their progress. Improving your* *weak points, however, will never let you get into flow state. Only your talents can do that. It's quite obvious – if you are not particularly good at something, you're constantly afraid of failure and can't immerse yourself fully in the present moment. Look at me, for example: I am extremely bad at drawing. If I was given years of intensive tutoring comparable to that received by Leonardo da Vinci, would it actually turn me into Leonardo? Of course it wouldn't.*

Modern technology allows teachers to put Comenius' theories into practice, letting the children experience everything they couldn't otherwise try out or imagine within the school environment. Technology can also be used to help children with special needs. Unfortunately, even though things like tablets, interactive whiteboards, and other gadgets are readily available, standard schools don't have much use for them.

TEACHER TYPOLOGY

The "school by play" method requires an involved, enthusiastic teacher. We have created a teacher typology,[8] which includes four different types of teacher. You probably remember the first three types from your own school days. Finding the rare fourth type means a true blessing for your child.

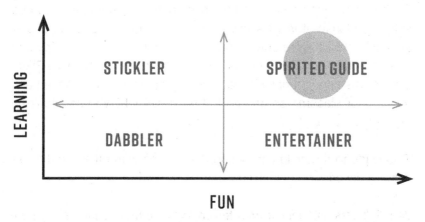

The vertical axis represents learning – information and knowledge which the teacher imparts to children in school. The horizontal axis indicates how fun the teacher can make the learning process.

DABBLER

This type of teacher does not give children enough relevant information. They teach children the bare minimum, without any personal contribution whatsoever, and children are bored. Dabblers are teachers without any talent for teaching, and their teaching process is highly unsuitable. No sane parent would wish for such a teacher for their child.

STICKLER

The Stickler type is slightly better than a Dabbler. They provide children with useful information, albeit using the wrong method. They try to drum knowledge into children's heads through memorizing. Children remember the information for a limited time but soon forget what they have learned.

ENTERTAINER

Entertainers are definitely better teachers than both Sticklers and Dabblers. The only difference, however, is that their lessons are usually fun and children enjoy them. They try to make the classes entertaining or even downright comical, but children do not learn much. Entertainers are not much use education-wise, but at least children enjoy their classes. You may once have had such a teacher yourself. You probably remember them fondly, but remembering anything they taught you? Not so much.

SPIRITED GUIDE

A Spirited Guide is an ideal type of teacher who can both impart knowledge and make children retain it. They help students establish an emotional connection with the learning material (teaching history through stories, for example). Children have to study hard, but classes are fun and enjoyable.

Jan: *Learning can't be entirely easy; children need to work and make an effort. However, once they manage to establish an emotional connection – either to the teacher or the learning material – they will remember what they have learned for the rest of their life. It works just like that in the professional world. If a manager is able to function as a "Spirited Guide," employees will work hard but still enjoy what they are doing. A great example of such a manager is Richard Branson, English business magnate and founder of the Virgin Group.*

An official study conducted by Charles University[9] found that 77 percent of students attending the Faculty of Education were not even considering working with children in future. These are alarming statistics which explain why there are so many Dabblers among schoolteachers. Sadly, many students who enter schools of education have absolutely no intention of actually teaching. They either see such schools as an easy way to a college degree or have no idea which college to go to and take advantage of the relatively easy entrance exams. Some might resign themselves to actually going into teaching, but they hardly consider it their dream job. Some of the graduates may try teaching in elementary schools but end up as Dabblers due to their general lack of enthusiasm. They usually stick with teaching for lack of other options.

Still, there are many great teachers out there, as well as many interesting educational methods. One of them is the much-discussed Hejny Method – a non-traditional way of teaching mathematics, created by Professor Milan Hejny, a Czech mathematician and leading expert in mathematical didactics. His method is currently taught at 30 percent of Czech elementary schools. It teaches children that problems can be solved in many different ways and offers them various options. Making children find their own solutions supports creative thinking.

Shell Oil Company conducted a survey, asking a single fundamental question: What does a company need in order to remain among the top five in its field for over 200 years? The results were clear: the only true competitive edge was a company's ability to learn new things quickly and effectively. Obviously, this is only possible if the company's employees are capable of fast learning, and you can't learn fast and effectively if you are permanently under stress. As we have discussed, the best possible results can be achieved in flow state. This means that companies that allow people to work in flow and utilize their talents to the maximum will gain a great competitive edge. Technologies, processes, strategy, customers, partners – all of those can be copied or stolen. The only truly unique thing is the people's talents and their ability to use them. A company with a manager capable of creating high-functioning teams where all members are able to utilize their talents will be able to compete with anyone in its field and maintain its competitive advantage in the long run.

Jan: *I believe that only companies capable of inducing and maintaining flow state in their employees can achieve long-term success. It works in virtually any field – sports, business, arts, anything we do.*

Unfortunately, most companies do the exact opposite: they focus too much on boosting their employees' weaknesses and fail to utilize their valuable talents. As part of a quarterly/annual assessment, employees are informed of their shortcomings and weaknesses, and receive recommendations as to which areas they need to improve. Companies are convinced that once employees manage to master their weaknesses, they will turn into true corporate champions. That's not how it works – not in sports, and certainly not in business. In an effort to improve their weak points, people stop focusing on their strengths – and become entirely average. Schools and businesses fail to utilize people's talents. Research has shown that only about 13 percent of people actually use their innate talents in their job. That's quite a sad number.

At our workshops and in this book, we try to emphasize the importance of talents and aptitudes for a person's life and encourage parents and children to identify and develop those talents, instead of trying to improve weaknesses.

3

TECHNOLOGY AND THE FAST-CHANGING WORLD

Up until now, humankind has been living in a linearly developing world. The human race's progress, inventions, and developments have been happening in increments. Some 50 years ago, Intel founder Gordon Moore made an observation that the number of transistors in a dense integrated circuit doubles about every 18 to 24 months, now known as **Moore's law**. In effect, this means that global computing capacity over that period doubles, which has vast consequences both for the global economy and the human brain. The brain's function has not changed for millennia, and it functions linearly, just as it did 10,000 years ago. It is therefore in no way prepared for the bi-annual doubling. Whenever you are pushed out of your comfort zone, your Monkey (the amygdala, Chapter 1) activates the "fight-or-flight" response. There is no alternative option or a middle ground.[10] In our distant past, which has programmed these responses into our brain, you could either try to fight the animal attacking you or run away from it, so the "fight-or-flight" response was actually very useful. In today's world, however, we need our brains to stop operating in a linear manner and start functioning exponentially, taking advantage of the exponential development enabled by **modern technology**. In a single week, our brains need to process more information than our ancestors received during their entire life. This extreme pressure actually compresses time: problems that required an hour of your time two years ago now have to be squeezed into half an hour. The time compression proceeds ever faster – in the future, our pace will have to speed up exponentially.

Both children and adults are under enormous pressure. In prehistoric times, periods of extreme stress might have occurred perhaps once a month, when it was time to go hunting. In today's rat race, such stressful moments can easily come once every ten minutes. Advances in technology have reduced our stress caused by imminent physical danger but have increased our mental stress, which is often far worse.

Things keep changing at an exponential pace, but our Monkey still works just as it did a thousand years ago. It insists on warning us of every possible failure, and the more we feel pressured by the fast-paced modern life, the more it keeps acting up. As the volume of information grows exponentially, so does the pressure we are under. Competition is fierce in all fields of business, made even more difficult by the fact that instead of competing locally, people now have to compete on a global scale.

(If your job is driving a snowplow, you probably won't be overly affected by global competition. Even though it is certainly an important job, it is tied to your local community. However, if you start working for a business or even a large corporation, you will find yourself a part of the global market.[11])

One of the contributing factors of the extremely fast spread of the 2008 global financial crisis was the internet. Any information posted online can instantly cause worldwide repercussions. Shortly before the crisis broke out, people read the news about the stock exchange collapse and started panicking and selling their stock as quickly as they could, which caused the entire economy to crash. Similar factors then prompted the economy to restore itself again. Such situations can be very dangerous.[12]

In order to be able to cope with the world created by modern technology, and to see it as an opportunity rather than a threat, we need to improve our mental hygiene and self-awareness. Unfortunately, schools have not taught us how to do either of these things (nor do they teach them to our children). Many people have no idea that such concepts even exist, let alone how to use them. We are not aware of their importance until we are in trouble.

Digital technologies offer **great opportunities**. Thanks to them, anyone – children, young people, and adults alike – can learn from the greatest educators in the world, through such channels as YouTube, the LinkedIn network, or various educational courses and websites (MOOC, Khan Academy,[13] etc.). However, technology also includes old-school audio recordings, which parents tend to overlook even though they used to like them very much when they were little. Children respond to stories played from a CD differently than if they simply watched them on a tablet, computer monitor, or TV screen. Listening to the spoken voice, children can engage their creative side by forming the images in their mind (similar to reading a book). They can let their other senses rest, close their eyes, and immerse themselves in the world of their imagination.

Kateřina: *I used to love audio recordings when I was little. I started by listening to children's books and plays and quite quickly proceeded to famous comedy skits and plays. I listen to these even today, from time to time. At nine years old, I was obviously too young to understand every single joke, but I certainly started to appreciate them later on, as I gained more experience and knowledge. Listening to the spoken word allows children to use their imagination but also practice their ability to concentrate, focus, and understand the context.*

Suggestion: Find time to listen to the spoken word with your child. You can listen to audio books and recordings in the car, but it's even better to reserve some special time just for listening, for example, during the afternoon siesta or before bedtime. Make yourself comfortable, let go of all your inner worries and concerns, cuddle up with your child, and listen to a story. You can turn it into a sort of ritual, just for the two of you.

Technology can also play a positive role in the learning process, fulfilling **three important functions**.

- Technology can assist children in **individual learning**, tailored to their specific needs and talents. For children (students, adults) who are predominantly visual learners, Khan Academy offers learning programs based on visual stimuli. Logical learners can try mathematical programs offering various logical exercises.

- Thanks to modern technology, learning has become a **global process**. With English being the universal language of international communication, once a child from any part of the world learns to speak English, they can interact with their peers from all over the world.

Jan: *My daughter attended several international schools. Whenever she was trying to solve a problem, she wouldn't come to me; instead, she simply turned on Skype. Within minutes, she put together a team of five children from four different continents, and they looked for a solution together.*

- **Teamwork** is going to become an important part of the learning process. Modern technology takes down the barriers between people, places, and ideas. Thanks to social media and modern communication tools, such as Skype, children will have to learn to work in teams. Teamwork is turning out to be an essential skill which is not yet adequately taught and practiced in schools. Individual learning and testing are of course still necessary, but supporting students to work together as a team is equally important. With the aid of modern technology, students can solve problems in a flexible manner, work together online, and instantly share their ideas and the files required for team projects.

Jan: *Many psychologists consider the Western model of society, focusing on the needs of the individual, superior to the collectivist Asian model. I believe that we should strive to achieve some kind of middle ground and embrace some aspects of the Asian collectivist cultures. There's no need to set up a special committee for every single decision, but learning to work as a team is important. If you are not a team player, you either need to learn fast or you will probably fail in almost every job. All the "big projects" today are created by teams: from a small team of doctors and nurses performing an operation to teams of some 30,000 software engineers writing code for Microsoft or Google. The team leaders' task is to put together the right people and steer them in the right direction, in order to create synergy and achieve a flow state – not only as individuals but as a whole team.*

DIGITAL HYGIENE

The use of technology is closely related to digital hygiene. You should NEVER underestimate digital hygiene, both physical (staying offline as much as possible) and mental. If you want your brain to function effectively and consistently, even under stress, you need to give your mind plenty of regular rest.

Today's children are the first generation to have been born in the digital age, surrounded by technology at every turn – which means that we have no idea what kind of impact the ever-present technology is going to have on them. They are perfectly able to handle cell phones, tablets, and computers from an early age, but there is no way to tell how they are going to function when they are 30 or 40 years old, both relationship - and career-wise.

Technology-induced mental stress can lead to various attention disorders. Today's children are often described as "over-informed but under-focused" – overloaded by information and unable to concentrate.

A brain under stress tends to jump from one thing to another, which closes the paths to the subconscious and long-term memory. People unable to focus for a prolonged period tend to have learning problems.

"Digital Dementia"[14] is a term coined by neuroscientist Manfred Spitzer to describe the breakdown of cognitive abilities due to the overuse of digital technology. Spitzer claims that as many as 30 percent of today's children are going to have learning problems in the future. A person incapable of long-term focus and concentration cannot be educated because they are unable to grasp the connections between various concepts. People today are only capable of 11 minutes of continuous focus, which is exceptionally poor.

Jan: *I believe that people capable of prolonged periods of concentration will earn a lot of money in the future. In fact, the inability to focus and pay attention costs a lot of money even now. In the US, attention disorders claim the second largest share of the healthcare budget, just after obesity.*

It is inevitable that today's children will come into contact with modern technology; there's no use keeping them in a protective bubble. Virtually everyone has a cell phone, laptop, or PC. It would make no sense to behave as if those devices don't exist. Instead, parents should focus on improving their own digital hygiene and become a good role model for their children in this respect. There's no use shielding children from technology; you will do them a much better service if you don't spend every waking moment attached to your smartphone.

Suggestion: Start to apply the principles of digital hygiene when you spend time with your children. If you take your children out to dinner but spend half the time checking your e-mail or Facebook on your phone, you are not setting them a good example. Once you actually manage to tear yourself off your smartphone, you shouldn't be surprised that your children no longer want to talk to you, glued to their own phones or tablets. If you're not able to stick to your own rules, how can you enforce them with your children?

Digital technology has its clear benefits, and to a certain extent we are all dependent on it. However, it's important to make a conscious effort to detach yourself from your devices regularly, and make sure your children see and copy what you are doing.

Jan: *A few years back, I predicted that more and more top managers would come from Asia in the future – and I was right. The reason is simple: managers from Eastern cultures are far more resistant to stress than* *their Western counterparts. I used to work in top management for 22 years myself and know all too well the pressure managers are under. The constant stress requires an ability to relax and recharge on a regular basis.*

Suggestion: Explain to your children how to use digital technology. Here are some of the things you should discuss:

- how to use digital technology, for how long, and how often;

- how to utilize technology for both entertainment and learning;

- when it's better to use a tablet, smartphone, or computer and when it's preferable to put them away.

Don't let technology get in the way of quality time spent with your loved ones. Share an activity or a meal, have a nice talk, or play a game. Try to avoid picking up your phone, calling someone, or checking your e-mail during this time. Set an example to your children.

Parents often use technology as a crutch when they have no idea how to spend time with their children. Sitting them down in front of the television or tablet seems a great way to keep the child occupied. Rather than patiently explaining to the child what they can or cannot do, parents give them a device to entertain themselves. Such an approach, however, fails to set up the boundaries a child will need in the future.

Mental hygiene recommendations

- stay away from all digital devices from time to time

- train to improve your focus and attention span

- focus on the present moment as often as possible and concentrate on your own breathing

- meditate

- relax mentally

When a child is bored or throws a tantrum, parents often try to appease them with digital devices to entertain them or calm them down.

Think about it this way: there is nothing wrong with a child being bored from time to time. That happens. You do not need to keep your child entertained every minute of the day. A child should be able to experience boredom or tedium and learn how to handle such situations. Adults often have to spend time in dull and tedious meetings or conferences, listening to things they find boring. Besides, there are many options to keep a child occupied other than a tablet or smartphone.

Kateřina: *At our workshops, there are moments when children take turns participating. Some have to wait patiently for their turn. We often use motivational coloring pictures for such a purpose. Children who are unable to simply sit and listen can try coloring. This works extremely well – children can color and listen to other children or parents talking. They can still take in everything that's going on, without needing a smartphone to keep them quiet and occupied.*

As a parent, you can explain to your child: "We're just going to sit here for an hour and listen to some interesting things. If you're bored, you can draw or color." Drawing/coloring does not distract the child from reality as much as a game or video on a tablet would.

Children often only act up because they find themselves in a boring situation and are trying to find some kind of distraction. Once the parent explains why this has to happen and that they need to pay attention for a while, most children can focus quite quickly. Sometimes all a parent needs to do is just touch the child gently to help them calm down and start paying attention again.

Technology can be extremely distracting for today's children; however, we are convinced that nothing, not even the most sophisticated digital device, can beat a good story.

Kateřina: *Sometime in the late 1990s, when I was about the same age as the children attending our workshops, the first sophisticated computer games and cell phones appeared. Even though they were nowhere near the technology surrounding children today, they were still extremely distracting. Some experts at the time claimed that printed books were a thing of the past and that future generations would no longer find reading interesting. And guess what happened then? The Harry Potter books came out! I read the first book when I was about ten years old. It completely enchanted me and brought me back to reading. I grew up with Harry, just like today's children do. A good story can remain popular for years, even decades, and still has the power to keep children away from computer screens and cell phone displays.*

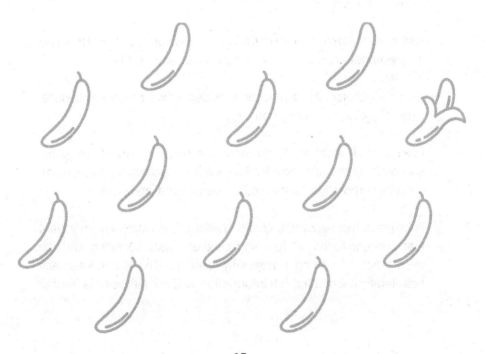

[1] Source: Jan Mühlfeit, Melina Costi (2016). *The Positive Leader.* FT Press.

[2] It takes about 21 to 30 days of training and repetition for an activity to become ingrained.

[3] Source: http://www.braingym.org

[4] Source: http://www.playwisely.com

[5] Source: Andrew Fuller (2015). *Unlocking Your Child's Genius: How to Discover and Encourage Your Child's Natural Talents*. Finch Publishing.

[6] From an interview given by Radkin Honzák for the Czech television talk show *Hyde Park*, broadcast on 7 April 2018.

[7] This is the method used by Montessori schools, Waldorf schools, and other progressive education systems.

[8] We created the teacher typology based on the teachings of John Amos Comenius.

[9] Source: http://www.lidovky.cz/rada-pedagogu-uci-blbe-i-20-let-dgm-/zpravy-domov.aspx?c=A170422_133644_ln_domov_ELE

[10] Some psychologists have recently added a third possible response, "freeze" (doing absolutely nothing).

[11] Even a small, local family business can become part of the global economic system if it provides its services or goods to a large, multi-national corporation. Global scale means global competition.

[12] Fake news has become a global problem. It is extremely important that schools focus on teaching children critical thinking and the importance of finding trustworthy sources. The exponential age has literally flooded us with information, and sometimes it is hard to

distinguish – especially for children – between the really relevant news and questionable sources.

[13] Khan Academy is an educational website offering online lessons in various fields, both for students and adults.

[14] Source: Manfred Spitzer (2012). *Digitale Demenz: Wie wir uns und unsere Kinder um den Verstand bringen.*

Part 2:

FROM SELF-AWARENESS TO FLOW

4

SELF-
AWARENESS

To help children find and unlock their potential, you need to start with yourself first. You must first learn to know yourself (self-awareness): only then can you start believing in yourself (self-confidence) and be aware of your own value (self-worth). Once you achieve all of these stages, you can start putting them into practice (self-expression). Only then can you be happy with yourself, become a role model both for your children and other adults, and help others by sharing your experience so that they can develop their own self-awareness, strengths, and talents.

Jan: *At my coaching workshops for top managers and CEOs, I am often asked to help raise a participant's self-confidence. That is an absurd request, however; you cannot be self-confident if you don't truly know yourself. You will not automatically start trusting a random person you meet in the street; you need to get to know them first. People tend to assume that since they've been here a while, they must know themselves pretty well by now. That is a common misconception. To build up your self-confidence, you first need to discover your strengths and weaknesses. Self-awareness is the key to self-confidence.*

At Wimbledon, the top ten players commonly train with players ranking hundreds of places below them. Watching such a training match, you probably wouldn't be able to tell who the better-ranking player is. The real game is where it shows – a true champion knows their strong and weak points and can get into and stay in flow state at will. The lower-ranking player can occasionally achieve flow but has no idea how to keep it going.

Anyone can learn how to get into flow state and stay in it. All you need to do is get to know yourself. Self-awareness is crucial for achieving flow state, discovering your talents, and maintaining mental and digital hygiene, as well as for your success and happiness. Unfortunately, self-awareness is not a subject commonly taught in schools, and for many people it may prove an insurmountable challenge. Getting to know yourself is never a waste of time.

Only people who truly understand themselves can succeed in any endeavor. The human brain is wired for survival, not success; therefore, it keeps alerting us to possible failures and warning us to be careful and not take unnecessary risks. This concept is easy to understand, but not everyone is aware of it. It causes us to fret over insignificant things instead of focusing on areas in which we can succeed. Unfortunately, traditional education systems do not allow students to explore their talents; instead, they focus on eliminating weaknesses. This approach then carries over to the professional sphere.

GENERAL APPROACH TOWARD A CHILD'S DEVELOPMENT

Parents of schoolchildren devote very little time to improving the subjects their child does well and spend up to ten times as long focusing on those the child does poorly. This means that they spend ten times longer on things their child will never have a chance to succeed in.

As a society, we focus on improving weaknesses. Both parents and teachers encourage children to merely preserve their strengths but eliminate their weaknesses, believing that they are giving them a chance to grow and improve. The idea that eliminating one's weaknesses can lead to success and happiness is a gross misapprehension. Working on your weak points will help you prevent failure, but only your strengths can lead you toward happiness and success.

The story of a little rabbit is an illustration of the 21st-century attitude toward human talent.

THE STORY OF A LITTLE RABBIT

On his first day of school, little rabbit came home overjoyed: there was a jumping competition, and he won a gold medal. His mother was happy for him and asked him how the competition went and what he liked best about it. The next day, little rabbit went to school all excited. When he came home, he was happy again but not as happy as he had been the previous day. His school had a running competition, and he came in third. On his third day of school, little rabbit came home in tears, so devastated he wouldn't even talk to his mother. The next day, he finally confided in her. The school had a swimming contest, and he came in last. "That's all right," his mother said, "I'm not mad at you." Still, little rabbit wouldn't stop crying. Finally, his mother got him to explain. "The teacher told me that since I finished last, all I would be doing from now on was swimming," he sobbed.

STRENGTH-BASED APPROACH

Knowing your own weaknesses is an essential part of self-awareness. However, weaknesses are not nearly as important as your strengths. Instead of discovering what a person is, we explore what they aren't. Realizing and reversing this trend – both on an individual level and as a society – will allow us to focus on people's talents and authentic strengths. Instead of average or below-average teams, we will have top-level teams on a global scale.

Jan: *I managed to achieve this while working for Microsoft. From a below-average team, I built a team that ranked the best in the Microsoft group worldwide, four times in a row!*

To succeed, you need to be yourself and use your natural talents and aptitudes. However, the only person who can make you be yourself is you.

"Do I want to be myself or not?"

That is a decision only you can make. If you decide not to try to be yourself, or if you never even ask yourself the question, you become a copy of someone else. That's why 87 percent of people today have a job that does not make them happy.[15] However, it's not rocket science: you simply need to utilize people's inner potential to the maximum.

Self-awareness is the most important factor for success and happiness. We have decided to express it by this simple motto:

Be more of who you are.

> **Suggestion:** Be as much of yourself as you can; others can always tell if you're not.

Historically, body language evolved long before the spoken word, and humans are far more sensitive to it. People are capable of detecting false behavior within approximately 17 milliseconds! This effect is known as *incongruence*: non-verbal gestures and facial expressions tell us that the person we are talking to is not genuine, that they are pretending to be something they are not. People who are simply being themselves, without the need to lie or pretend, don't have to watch their body language. They are predictable and believable. (Of course, that doesn't mean that they are also automatically likable.)

Life is too short for us to content ourselves with being average, or even below average. Most people who have had tremendous success had to make a choice and break out of the system. They stopped being part of the crowd and chose their own way. Who cares that Bill Gates, once the richest man in the world, did not graduate from college? The richest man in Britain, Richard Branson, did not even finish high school. As a dyslexic, he struggled in the traditional education system, which did not allow him to study at the pace and in the way he needed. Instead, he chose to develop his strengths on his own, outside the school system.

In school, teachers will often tell you that "there is only one way to learn this" (whatever "this" may be). If a student fails to grasp the subject using the required methods, they will fail. In the professional environment, you will commonly hear that "as a division manager/ CEO/marketing manager, you need to do things this way." In fact, there is no wrong way of doing things, provided that it works. Mount Everest can be climbed from more than one side, and tasks can be accomplished in more than one way. The same subject can be grasped and learned through various methods. Different personality types respond to different learning methods: logical thinkers need logical tools; visual learners require a lot of visual stimuli. Some students have a better memory, others, a better power of deduction. Digital technology may help children learn things using various methods, depending on their particular needs. Unfortunately, not many schools use digital technology in this manner; again, they tend to stick with the method they consider to be the "right" one.

We use various visual exercises to demonstrate the principles of innovative thinking to children. You can try solving the following problems with your children.

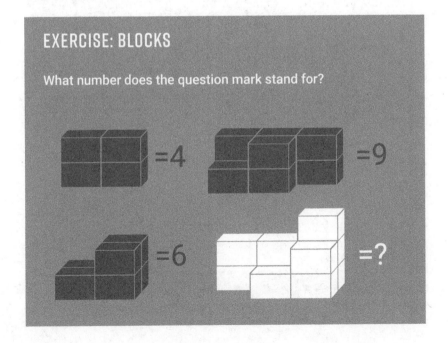

EXERCISE: BLOCKS

What number does the question mark stand for?

=4

=9

=6

=?

Solution: 10.

Always ask your children what method they used to solve the problem. "I just did it; the result is 10" is not a good enough answer. Everyone's reasoning is a little different and it's good to reflect on it.

Some people may simply count the blocks to see whether the number next to the equal sign really corresponds to the number of blocks. It's usually adults who don't automatically trust the numbers, thinking it might be a trick question. Children are mostly trusting enough to simply start counting the blocks in the last picture.

You could also optically rearrange the blocks into a simpler shape to make it easier to count them.

You can also compare the last picture to the one directly above it. You will realize that the pictures are nearly identical. Just move the front section a little toward the right and add an additional block. 9 + 1 = 10.

Now look at this picture.

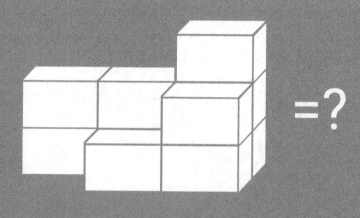

Don't try to fit it into the logical sequence. Just think about the number of blocks. Ask yourself (and your child) whether the result really has to be 10. Could there be another solution or explanation?

Solution:

The result could be 9. We cannot see one of the blocks, so we have no way of knowing whether it's really there. There could be a gap, with the block right above it glued to the adjoining blocks.

The result could be 11, or even 12. We can't see what's behind the second row of blocks; there could easily be another block or two hiding there.

Some blocks might even be buried in the ground, so there is really an infinite number of solutions.

The exercise is not about finding all possible solutions. It's designed to make you think about other alternatives and be able to explain and defend them.

Could you or your child come up with another solution?

EXERCISE: MATCHES

The problem uses Roman numerals – a six, a two, and a five. Move a single match so that the problem makes sense.

Solution:

If you take the vertical match from the plus sign and add it to the first number, you will now have VII − II = V.

Taking the vertical match from the plus sign and adding it to the number after the equal sign will get us VI − II = IV.

Those are the two basic solutions. Most children or students will have no problem figuring them out. However, try to ask them whether there could be other solutions. You might give them a hint: "The instructions say nothing about there having to be an equal sign." Taking away any vertical match (i.e., not the ones forming the equal sign) and placing it aslant across the equal sign will get us VI − II ≠ V.

You could also make an unfinished problem by turning the equal sign into a plus sign: VI + II + V

You can also remove one match from the equal sign and put it anywhere else, so the equal sign will now become a minus sign: VI + III − V or VI + II − IV etc.

These exercises are meant to demonstrate that there doesn't always have to be a single correct solution.

Suggestion: Always try to be creative. Ask yourself or your children: "Could there be another way to solve this?"

PARENTING STYLES

It is important for parents to get to know themselves and define their relationship with their children. Parents should also determine what they actually want to teach their children. Only after you discover yourself and your own talents can you help your children explore theirs.

At our workshops, *Unlocking a Child's Potential* and *Parent as a Positive Coach*, we meet many different parents and get to consult them on the real-life challenges they are facing as parents. Based on countless interviews, we have defined four basic parenting categories.

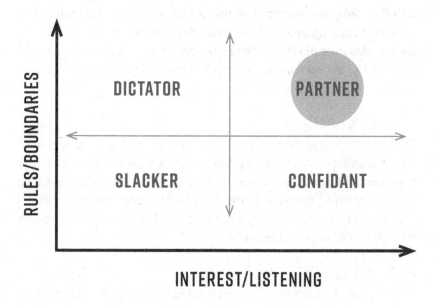

The vertical axis describes the boundaries each type of parent sets for their children, and the horizontal axis shows the degree of the parent's involvement and empathy.

SLACKER PARENT

Slackers have a lackadaisical attitude toward parenting, setting their children no rules and boundaries whatsoever. Some might actually be popular with their children, since they don't nag or bother; unfortunately, they also don't bother to listen when their child actually needs them.

DICTATOR PARENT

Dictators are strict parents who set firm rules and boundaries. They are not interested in actually listening to their child. "You're going to do what I say. I am the one who sets the rules around here," is their motto. Sometimes a specific situation may require that a parent assume the Dictator role for a while, but it should never be long term: ideally, we should strive to stay in the Partner parent box.

Kateřina: *My great-grandmother was a typical Dictator. My mother had actually picked up some of her parenting methods from her, but she always tried to be our Partner and Confidant, too – mostly whenever she realized she did not want to be a carbon copy of her grandmother, who had been very strict with her.*

CONFIDANT PARENT

Confidants listen to their children, but they are not big on setting rules and boundaries. This category often includes divorced parents who only spend the occasional weekend with their child and try to make it up to them by letting them run loose. The children know that their parents care about them, but with no boundaries and limits they do whatever they want – which is not good.

PARTNER PARENT

Partners are ideal parents. They set the rules, but they also observe how the child reacts to them. Together, they can adjust the rules to suit both sides. Having rules and boundaries is necessary, but parents don't have to be the only ones setting them. A parent can react flexibly to whatever the child tries to tell them and to any situations that may arise. If a parent is interested in their child and knows how to listen to them, the child will absorb and imitate this pattern of behavior. The parent and child will become partners, and both will be equally happy in their relationship. Communication, listening, and mutual respect are the key.

As parents, we may often move from one box to another: we are only human, and sometimes even the best parent loses their temper. However, one of the quadrants usually tends to be dominant.

Sometimes a parent finds it necessary to change quadrants on purpose, using an approach known in the business sphere as situational leadership.

If a child keeps acting up, testing their boundaries, or getting into dangerous situations, parents need to be stricter and set the limits, without trying to bargain with the child or persuade them. Once the child has calmed down and is open to rational discussion, the parent can again become a Partner.

Parents at our workshops often tell us that before they had children, they were firmly resolved not to repeat their own parents' mistakes. Now they've actually become parents, they constantly find themselves shouting at their children and ordering them around. They are exhausted and unable to truly listen to their children, then feel guilty about it and feel that they failed as a parent.

The following steps can help you become the kind of parent you want to be.

HOW TO BECOME A PARTNER PARENT

- **In any situation, you can take a step back and realize that you might be doing something you don't want to do.** You might have just given your child a stern dressing-down, and they're crying. Do you really want to make your own child cry? Most parents will say that they definitely don't. Don't keep your feelings to yourself. Tell your child how you feel. "Look how we're treating each other right now," you could say. "I've been yelling at you and now you're crying. Neither of us is happy. Let's talk about it and see if we can do things differently next time so this won't happen again." Whenever you have this realization and act on it, you're one step closer to becoming a Partner.

- You should regularly ask yourself: **Am I in the right parent category?**
  If not, then ask yourself some more questions: What am I doing wrong? Or what is my child doing wrong? We both want to become partners. What can I do about it? How can I help my child meet me halfway?

- **Stop striving for perfection. Don't be afraid to lose your temper in front of your child.** Things can't always be perfect. You might be tired after a long day of work, exhausted by your child constantly pestering you or testing their boundaries. You might lose your temper from time to time, and that won't be pleasant for either one of you. However, if you keep your anger bottled up, pretending that everything is hunky-dory, or if you keep shutting yourself in the next room to recharge and restore your positive attitude, you might be heading toward something far worse than a simple emotional outburst. Even a very small child can handle it if you're not able to keep your cool at all times. They will pick up your patterns of behavior and if you show your feelings and emotions, they will find it natural to express their own feelings and emotions. Sometimes you may think that children are too young to

82

understand their parents' problems. Children are sensitive, however, and often they are able to sense your bad mood and calm down. Sometimes they might even give you a hug or a kiss, or even put their reaction into words: "It's gonna be alright, Mom." "I'll never hit my sister again, I promise."

- **Give your child a chance to participate in setting the rules –** within limits determined by you as a parent, of course. If your child keeps acting up at every turn, disrespecting the rules you've set despite your constant reminders, try to shift some of the responsibility for establishing the rules to the child. Instead of being constantly annoyed and telling the child off ("How many times have I told you not to jump up and down on the couch?"), take a deep breath and ask your child to try and find a solution. "Do you think you could try jumping somewhere else where you might enjoy it just as much?" "Can you think of anything we can do so we'll both be happy and we won't break the furniture?"

- **Show your child that you are sympathetic toward their feelings and emotions, and try to define them together.** Imagine that you're at a playground. Another boy's mother is mad at you because your son kicked hers in the leg. How do you respond? Do you reprimand your child straight away? "Why did you do that? Do it again and we'll be going straight home!" Or will you perhaps try to find out what really happened? Your son might explain: "That other kid stomped on my beautiful sandcastle, and he wouldn't apologize, so I kicked him." You may think your son's reaction was inappropriate – but even so, try to show him that you understand his anger. You might get really angry yourself sometimes; the only difference is that you're an adult, and you can control your emotions better. You could try saying to your son: "I'm sure you must have been really mad at him to have kicked him so hard. I guess the sand castle took a lot of work? And he ruined it, right?" Your son might start talking about the whole incident: "He made me so mad! You don't do a thing like that! He deserved it." At this point, there's no need to tell him that his reaction was over-the-top; he will most likely realize it himself. What he needs from you is your sympathy and understanding. He needs you to listen and show him that you know how he feels. Sometimes, all you need to do is nod; in the end, your child will realize that he might have overreacted. You could remind him of the Monkey, who is usually responsible for such fits of temper. In the end, your child will find out that you can only control such emotions as anger, fear, or nervousness if you can identify and understand them.

- **Try to slow down and simply be together.** In today's fast-paced world, it is hard to just enjoy the moment. You don't always need to have a special program prepared to entertain your child. Sometimes all you need to do is just stop and simply be there for your child – here and now. Your child may be fascinated with ants crawling up a tree, a puddle in the shape of an elephant, or even a simple daisy flower – but you're in too much of a hurry, trying to get them to school on time, to stop. You're late as it is, and you still have to go grocery shopping and answer a bunch of e-mails, and you don't have the time or the patience to just wade in a puddle. Do you still remember how such things used to captivate you when you were little, and how the adults would never understand – or perhaps they didn't want to? We may unwittingly miss many beautiful moments. Perhaps your child just wanted to tell you that the puddle looks like that elephant you saw on your vacation together and that they would very much like to go on another adventure with you. If only you could give them a moment, they might surprise you by how much they remember from that trip, even though they were only two years old at the time. Try to slow down and stop sometimes, and let your child show you the way into their world. Wait for them to pick up a flower – they're picking it to give to you anyway, to show you how much they love you. In a busy day or within a carefully planned program, there's no place for such little things.

You will find more tips on how to get one step closer to becoming a Partner in the next few chapters.

The following exercise allows children to improve their emotional intelligence by watching other people and trying to put themselves in their place.

EXERCISE: EMOTIONAL DETECTIVE

You can play this game virtually anywhere: out in the street, in the park, or at a bus stop. Discreetly point out a random passer-by to your child and ask them: "How do you think she is feeling right now?" The child can let their imagination run wild. If they don't know how to answer, you can try asking additional questions: "Do you think she's sad? Or happy? Or maybe angry?" Let the child decide which particular emotion best fits the person's expression.

After the child identifies a particular emotion, you can keep asking more questions. "Why do you think she's angry? Perhaps she had a bit of bad luck today?" Again, your child can use their imagination to guess what might have happened or will happen to the person. The exercise can turn into a fun game and quality offline time spent together. Together, you can make up stories behind the emotions you detect on people's faces.

For children aged 13 or older, this game probably won't work. Teenagers very much enjoy judging everyone and everything, but not in their parents' company. You can always give it a try though!

Kateřina: *When I used to go on vacation with my parents, my mother and I liked to guess things about other families we met. We particularly liked those who were somehow "different," i.e., not the standard "mom-dad-kids" type. Let's say we saw two women, three children, and an elderly gentleman. "Are the women sisters or best friends?" we would wonder. "And where are the kids' dads? Why couldn't they have come with them?*

Maybe they couldn't get off work? Or perhaps they're divorced? And who's the old man? Is he the kids' grandpa? Or maybe he's with one of the ladies?" We were not trying to be nosy or judgmental. It was a game of imagination: wondering about the various forms families could take, how they live, and so on. In fact, such a game can be a good exercise in tolerance and respect toward anyone who is "different."

JOHARI WINDOW[16]

INDIVIDUAL/SELF

	KNOWN TO SELF	UNKNOWN TO SELF
KNOWN TO OTHERS	**OPEN SELF** known talents and strengths **child + parents**	**BLIND SPOT** biased perceptions, misunderstanding, no self-regulation **parents**
UNKNOWN TO OTHERS	**HIDDEN SELF** undervalued, underutilized talent **child**	**UNKNOWN SELF** undiscovered potential **NOBODY**

OTHERS

HOW TO IMPROVE YOUR CHILD'S SELF-AWARENESS

The Johari window is a technique that helps people better understand themselves. It describes and categorizes a person's qualities and may help them discover their hidden potential. You can try using the Johari window with your children, adult family members, or friends, but also with your coworkers.

- The first window describes our "open self": qualities or abilities that both ourselves and other people are aware of – **things we know about ourselves and regularly show to others**.

- The second quadrant describes our "hidden self": qualities known to ourselves but not to others – **things we know about ourselves and hide from others**. We may sometimes uncover a part of our hidden self to others, deciding to share certain desires or qualities that only we know about. To become a true Partner to your child, let them know that they don't need to be afraid to share their hidden self with you – their desires, wishes, ideas, or troubles.

- The third window represents a "blind spot": qualities we are totally unaware of but that others know/perceive – **things we don't know about ourselves but other people do**. Feedback from others may help us discover our blind spot window. To explore it, you need to ask questions and try to reflect on them. What should I do next? What am I good at? What should I stop doing? Ask people what they think about you and encourage your child to do the same.

- The last quadrant represents the "unknown self": undiscovered potential that no one is yet aware of – **things neither you nor others know about yourself**. Psychometric tests involve open-ended questions which allow you to explore your undiscovered potential, effectively mapping your brain and revealing talents you may not be aware of. You can also explore your unknown self through one-on-one coaching sessions. They involve the coach asking open-ended questions, providing as little of their own insight and opinion as possible and helping the client explore their own personality. (More about coaching in Chapter 8: Parent as Positive Coach.)

Suggestion: Think about each of the four windows and try to fill them out. Ask your friends or family to help you with the quadrants which require the feedback and insight of others, or try completing a psychometric test. This may help you create a fairly complete picture of yourself.

DISCOVERING YOUR CHILD'S STRENGTHS AND WEAKNESSES

We are born with certain aptitudes, which are genetically programmed into our DNA. There is no way to change that – but, as in cards, when you've been dealt your hand, it's up to you how you play them.

Cyril Höschl: "Nature vs. nurture" is a question that natural science has been trying to answer for ages. Countless experiments and research programs have been devoted to it. There is an old book by Helen Grace Carlisle, *Mothers Cry*, first published in 1929. It tells of a simple, poor mother of several children. One of her sons was a successful architect; one of her daughters was killed – and another of her sons was the killer. Three children carrying the same set of genes, brought up by the same mother in the same environment, and their fates were completely different. If the parents' genetic information was the only determining factor, they would all have been very similar; and, conversely, if environment was the crucial factor of a child's development, three individuals brought up in the same environment would have developed similar personalities. However, genetic variations are endless, just as the environmental factors are, and the resulting combination ensures that no two individuals turn out exactly the same. Genetic traits may also skip a generation, so a son may take more after his grandfather than his father.

We all have certain aptitudes that influence the way we behave, communicate, and make decisions. Talents are not something only select people have. It's usually not hard to tell when someone has an aptitude for music, sports, or art: the ability to play the piano, paint a picture, or throw a fastball is very easy to spot and define. However, there are other types of talents we may not even be aware of: things like superb communication skills, reliability, empathy, leadership skills, and many others. It's extremely beneficial to learn to recognize them in yourself and consciously develop them. However, even the talents we may not yet be aware of can have a considerable impact on our behavior.

Kateřina: *We once had a pair of twins at our workshop – girls of about 11. They both looked identical, but it soon turned out they behaved very differently. We had them fill out an aptitude test and identified three talents for each of them, with the first two being the same. After we talked to their parents, it turned out that the girls were very competitive with one another. Siblings may fight or clash occasionally, but those two took it to extremes. This had a lot to do with the first two talents we identified in both of them – competitiveness and organizational skills. One was constantly trying to organize and outdo the other.*

The third talent, however, was different for each of the girls.

1. *I asked the first twin what kind of plans she had for the future. She told me she would soon be starting in a new school but was confident that everything would be just fine. She would like the school and make lots of friends. She didn't have any plans beyond that; having a lot of friends seemed to be the most important thing to her. Then she told me about the friends she had now and added that she liked the influence she had over them. She was apparently the leader of the group. She kept laughing and clowning around with another boy. Her third talent was the ability to influence others.*

2. *Her sister's answers to my questions were very sensible and well thought out. She wanted to be an architect, like her mother; she*

liked drawing and designing houses. She was already imagining what it would be like. She was wondering what the world would be like in a hundred years. Her third talent was the ability to see a clear vision of the future; she had great imagination and visualization skills.

The example of the twin girls illustrates that talents can sometimes be identified by the way a person acts and what they choose to share about themselves.

EXAMPLES OF POSSIBLE TALENTS

Communication skills

Empathy

Organizational skills

Strategic thinking

Creativity

Visionary skills

Analytical thinking

Ability to entertain

Adaptability

Inquisitiveness

Technical skills

Leadership skills

Competitiveness

Productivity

Proactive attitude

Adherence to principles

Ability to focus and concentrate

Positive attitude

Constructive thinking

Social networking skills

Ability to connect with people

Reliability

Responsibility

Ability to teach others

Patience

and many others ...

HOW TO DISCOVER YOUR CHILD'S TALENTS

Specialized psychometric tests are the best way to discover a person's aptitudes. There are many — mostly paid — variations of these tests available in English, each exploring a slightly different range of talents.

The following exercise is the simplest way to discover your child's (or your own) talents. (You can also try this exercise if you have already filled out a psychometric test but are not quite happy with the results.)

EXERCISE: DISCOVER YOUR TALENTS

Copy the following table onto a piece of paper — one for each of your children, and one for yourself. In the left column, include all activities that leave you/your children feeling energized (+). Children can usually recall many activities that are fun for them and make them happy. This is where the talents are hidden. We will later verify them by using five basic characteristics.

WHAT ENERGIZES ME	WHAT DRAINS ME OF ENERGY
things I like doing and things I am good at	things I do NOT like doing and things I am NOT good at
....	....
....	....
....	....
....	....

In the right-hand column, write down all activities that seem to drain you/your children of energy (−). This includes any activities children find exhausting or boring and that they are not particularly good at. This is where their weaknesses tend to be.

When testing your children, you might need to ask some leading questions to achieve meaningful results. You could try some of these:

How would you describe yourself in three short sentences?

How would your friends describe you in three short sentences? (feedback)

Which three things are you best at?

Which things can you learn faster than others?

Which activities make you the happiest?

Do you ever feel negative and unhappy with yourself? When does it happen?

Are there any things/activities you're finding particularly difficult?

WEAKNESSES

Focus on your strengths. Discover your talents. That's all we've been telling you so far. So why have we decided to start with discussing our weaknesses? The answer is simple – it's very important to discover both your strengths *and* weaknesses because they are both part of who you are. And it's far better to deal with weak points first – and leave plenty of space for discussing and exploring your talents.

IMPROVE YOUR WEAKNESSES
– BUT ONLY UP TO A POINT

Once you've written down all your weak points, try to accept them as a part of yourself. Seeing them put together like that may seem overwhelming, and you may feel like you will never amount to anything, no matter how hard you try. With such a mindset, however, you will never become a champion. Define your weaknesses and learn to accept them. You can say to yourself: "Those are my weak points. They are a part of me. I can always try to improve them to such a degree that they won't hinder me in developing my strengths."

Devoting too much of your energy to improving your weaknesses will only exhaust you. It is a slow process with many setbacks, and the most you can achieve is becoming average.

Parents and teachers tend to believe that children's true potential lies in improving their weak points. That is, however, a very unfortunate approach toward a child's development. Parents and/or educators content themselves with consolidating a child's strengths and focus most of their energy on areas in which the child is lacking in order to improve them. Focusing on improving weaknesses prevents failure – which must surely be a good thing, right? Nobody wants to fail.

For a child, failing a subject means repeating the school year. For an adult, failure could mean bankrupting their own company. Who would want that? We need to be aware of our weaknesses and try to improve them to a point where they won't cause us to fail or hinder our development.

However, the only road to success and happiness is to do what you like and what you're good at, utilizing and improving your strengths.

HOW TO DEAL WITH WEAKNESSES

If a child is weak in a certain subject and receives mostly Ds and Fs in it, they need to improve to at least a C grade if they want to complete both elementary and high school and perhaps even continue on to college. Bad grades can prevent them from studying what they like and what they're good at. A child should work hard to improve their weak subjects but harder still to improve those that they excel at.

Jan: *Personally, I wouldn't let a child spend more than 20 percent of their time on improving their weak points.*

> **Suggestion:** Use situational leadership and take into account your child's current standing.

- If a child's grades average between As and Bs, have them spend 90 percent of their time on improving their strengths and only 10 percent on their weaknesses.

- If a child manages relatively well in all of their subjects and is not downright failing in any of them, have them spend 80 percent of their effort and time working on their strengths, and devote 20 percent to bringing up their grades in their weakest subject to at least a C, so they can get through school with no major setbacks.

- If a child's grades are mostly Ds, or they are even failing a subject, the proportion needs to change dramatically. The child should spend only about 60 percent of their time working on their strengths and 40 percent on improving weaknesses. If the child's grades (or performance in sports) are suffering and their overall evaluation depends on them performing well in all of their subjects, it will be necessary to spend more time on building up their weak subjects to get them at least to a C grade – but only for a limited time. It's important to bring up a failing grade to at least a C, but not to an A – the child wouldn't be able to maintain it anyway.

It's important for parents to realize that even if the child is getting poor grades, they can still spend more time (60 percent) on developing their strengths than working on their weaknesses. Unfortunately, society's focus on improving weak points shifts this ratio to about 10:1. If a child consistently earns As in a subject, parents make them spend minimal time on that subject and make them devote most of their time to their weaker subjects. This ratio makes no sense and parents should consciously try to turn it around. Focus on strengths first and weaknesses second. Try to improve the child's weak subjects to a certain required level, but do not force them to put more effort into them than strictly necessary.

ELIMINATING WEAKNESSES THROUGH PARTNERSHIP

Besides knowing your weaknesses and balancing them with your strengths, it can also help to find someone who excels at those things you are not so good at. Perhaps they too have a weakness that is actually *your* strength. For most of their life, a person functions as part of a team: in their family, in school, in a relationship, in their job, in sports... Teams are simply everywhere. Sometimes they work well; sometimes not so much. When you're part of a team, you can use someone else's strengths to compensate for your weaknesses, and vice versa. That's how team cooperation actually works.

Parents should never forget that a family should also work as a team. Siblings are frequently competitive, constantly one-upping each other. Sibling rivalry often stems from the fact that parents and/or grandparents keep comparing the children's abilities. The children then constantly try to catch up with their siblings or outstrip them. It's far better to reassure your children that they don't need to fight for your attention by competing with their brother or sister. Fighting and competing is a normal part of children's games, but when they find themselves in a difficult situation, teach them to lean on their siblings' strengths and work as a strong team.

Kateřina: *My brother is three and a half years older than I am. We used to fight all the time when we were little, both verbally and physically. We even used to bite each other! But we could also work together when we needed to. When my mother scolded us for the mess in our room, we teamed up and got it tidied up faster. I did what I could, and my brother did the rest.*

When we wanted something but Dad was in a bad mood, my brother would always ask me to go talk to him. I was my dad's little girl and could always sit in his lap and talk him round. We joined forces like that quite often. When we were older and wanted to go out, my brother would always tell Mom he would take care of me so I wouldn't have to go home early. They trusted him to be responsible and let me stay out longer.

It's quite normal for people to be better at some things than you are. That doesn't mean that you are somehow inferior to them. Try to embrace this fact as part of your journey toward self-awareness, and teach it to your children as well.

TALENTS

If you excel at an activity, it comes easily and naturally to you. You feel happy and energized doing it, and improving it does not require as much effort as working on your weaknesses. Instead of getting stuck, you feel motivated and bursting with new ideas. Every obstacle is a challenge to improve.

Focusing on your talents makes you want to excel and strive for perfection.

ARE THOSE YOUR REAL TALENTS?

There are five basic characteristics that allow you to find out whether your child (or yourself) has an aptitude for a particular activity.

When you manage to discover which activities make you feel energized, you're on to something. The following characteristics will help you find out whether those activities which make you feel comfortable and energized are also your true talents.

FIVE BASIC CHARACTERISTICS CONFIRMING YOUR TALENTS[17]

DESIRE
A child (or an adult) engages in a particular activity on their own initiative, without being prompted to do so, simply because they want to. No one has to tell them: "Go do this. You have to try and get better at it." Obviously, children sometimes don't want to do anything at all, especially in adolescence, around age 11–14 or even later. Their hormones are in full swing, causing them to clash with their parents and

authorities in general in order to form their own adult personality. At this age, a child may refuse to do something, even if they actually want to do it, as a show of defiance against parental authority. Adolescent children therefore require a special approach. In general, however, if a child wants to do a particular activity on their own (apart from days when they're not in the mood), that particular activity is one of their talents.

Willingness, interest, and an urge to perform a particular activity are the key factors of desire.

Key question: Are there any activities toward which you feel a natural affinity?

FAST LEARNING
A child (or an adult) is able to master a particular activity or skill very quickly – faster than other activities.

Every child has a particular subject in school or a leisure activity they are able to master more quickly and efficiently than other subjects or activities, and they can do it faster than their peers or schoolmates. They don't need to revise for a particular subject, seemingly just soaking up the information. In sports, all they need is to be shown a particular move once to be able to do it. "Wow, this is easy," they think.

Key question: Is there an activity you've always been able to master very quickly?

INTUITION
A child (or an adult) can do something naturally and intuitively, without being instructed by a parent, teacher, or coach. They can quickly solve a math problem, paint a beautiful picture, or perform a nifty dodge in soccer. They know instinctively how a thing should be done and do it perfectly, even though no one has shown them how to do it before.

Key question: Are there any activities you've always been able to do, without being told how?

PERFECTION

A child (or an adult) performs a particular activity easily, surprising even themselves how well they can do it. They feel instinctively that it is something they are good at.

Key question: Have you ever performed a particular activity, realized you've done really well, and asked yourself how exactly you'd done it?

SATISFACTION

After performing a particular activity, a child (or an adult) may experience a feeling of satisfaction, knowing they've done well (either intuitively or with someone's instruction). They are looking forward to doing it again, and they are feeling energized and exhilarated.

Key question: Are there any activities which give you the feeling of satisfaction, either when you're doing them or afterwards? Do you look forward to doing them again?

If any of the activities or areas you (or your children) put down on your list as making you happy and energized intersect with the five characteristics we've just shared, they are definitely your talents.

> **Suggestion:** Try to think of something your child has done well in the past. Did they use any of their talents while doing it? Imagine your child having to make a decision in the future. Could their talents help them in some way?

When two children possess similar or identical talents, it doesn't necessarily mean they will both be suited for one particular job. They could utilize their talents in two entirely different fields, depending on what they like doing, what can get them in flow, and what they see as a meaningful life.

Conversely, two children with a completely different set of talents may excel in the same profession.

Let's say we have three children with the following talents:

JOE: managerial/technological type

Talents: imagination, organizational skills, eloquence

How can Joe's talents help him in a managerial position? Joe is a visionary thinker, and with his rhetorical skills, he is able to sell his visions to other people. Thanks to his organizational skills, he can also implement his visions, not merely talk about them.

DAVID: managerial/technological type

Talents: building relationships, analytical thinking, energetic personality

David would approach a managerial job quite differently. First, he would analyze what needs to be done. Thanks to his empathy and good people skills, he would build a great team. His energetic spirit would stimulate and motivate his employees.

Both boys would do well in the same job, but each would utilize a different set of talents to do it.

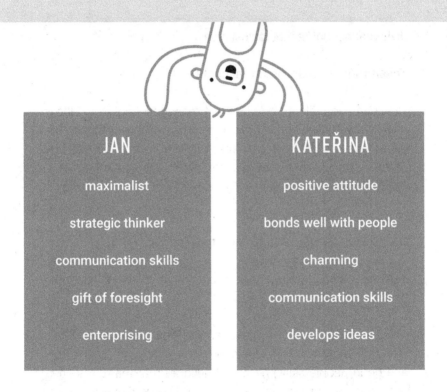

ANNIE: artistic type

Talents: imagination, organizational skills, eloquence

With her imaginative skills, Annie could become an actress or a show host. She could easily tune into her character, and her eloquence and rhetorical skills would help her perform the role convincingly. Organizational skills would help her both in learning her role and on stage.

JAN

maximalist

strategic thinker

communication skills

gift of foresight

enterprising

KATEŘINA

positive attitude

bonds well with people

charming

communication skills

develops ideas

Jan: *Maximalists are very demanding and hard to please, when it comes to both themselves and others. They always want to work with the best* *in the field. When you give them a rare pearl, they will immediately start polishing it.*

Strategic thinkers always think of various ways of doing things.

My communication skills probably come from my great-grandmother. I used to spend a lot of time with her when I was little. She listened to me and talked to me a lot. Around age five, I was able to rattle off jokes for more than half an hour straight.

People with the gift of foresight have great visualization skills, which manifest quite early in childhood. As a boy, I used to organize my own hockey tournaments in our hallway, using a small hockey stick and a ping-pong ball. I created entire teams, provided a running commentary on the games, and generally made a terrible racket. It drove my parents crazy, to the point that they sometimes broke my hockey stick... and then they had to buy me a new one because I just wouldn't stop begging.

Kateřina is an extremely positive, charming person, with great bonding skills. People with this talent can influence and lead others in a very positive way. They are very detail oriented. Think of Apple's Steve Jobs – his meticulousness was the reason Apple's devices were so perfectly designed, down to the last detail.

Kateřina and I each have slightly different talents, but we make a great team (two people are the smallest possible team unit). Besides doing our workshops and courses together, Kateřina also acts as my manager. I am not as detail oriented as she is, so it works out just fine.

BUILDING UP YOUR STRENGTHS

We are all born with certain talents. If you've done the DISCOVER YOUR TALENTS exercise, you may have identified and defined at least some of them, or you are about to. You may also feel like you have quite a few more talents than you thought, and something great and unexpected is about to happen in your life soon. Most of the time, however, nothing will.

That's because having a talent for something is not enough. Talent is only a potential that you first need to unlock – by investing an effort in developing it. Only then can you turn your talent into your strength.

How do we define a "talent"? A talent is a certain pattern of thinking, emotions, and behavior that can be explored and used productively.

The following simple but important equation explains how talents turn into strengths.

$$S \text{ (strength)} = T \text{ (talent)} \times I \text{ (investment)}$$

In this case, "investment" does not mean money but the effort, diligence, and time you put into developing your talent.

You can invest in your talents on two basic levels.

INVESTING INTO YOUR TALENTS

I. KNOWLEDGE

You can read books about your particular talent, search for information online, watch educational videos, films, and documentaries, or learn from friends/coworkers who specialize in that particular area. You may imagine the activities related to your talent and think about them. You may even try to visualize them. Practical activities are closely interlinked with your brain: success requires both doing and thinking about doing.

We teach visualization at our workshops, and you and your children may try it out using the exercise in Chapter 6.

If you have a dream, you first need to be able to imagine it. You have to become aware of what needs to be done to fulfill that particular dream, step by step, and get a sense of how it works and whether it is even possible.

It's sort of like learning to ride a bike: after days of practicing, you may dream about actually being able to do it. In the morning, you get on the bike – and realize you really *can* ride. Children need to learn that their mind is an important tool and that developing a certain talent also includes thinking about it.

You can do pretty much anything you are able to imagine clearly and in detail. If you can't imagine it, then you can't do it. Our subconscious is like a computer that constantly records data, without distinguishing between reality and projection. Imagine it as a garden: if you plant the right information and nurture it, it will grow into an achievement.

Today's athletes routinely spend only about 70 percent of their time in actual physical training. The remaining 30 percent is devoted to mental conditioning and visualization – in other words, simply imagining their achievements. Thinking about winning the Olympics puts you one step closer toward actually winning them.

The second level of investment into your talents requires developing your skills.

2. SKILLS

It is not enough to simply discover your talents and think about them – you need to put them into practice: in school, sports, playing with friends, in an after-school club...

Once a child starts putting their talents into practice, most likely they won't be perfect at first try. Making mistakes is normal. Parents should not scold their child for making a mistake, let alone mock them or get angry. Encourage your children not to be afraid of making mistakes while learning something; explain that they are simply a way to move forward and get better. Investing in a talent requires hard work, and mistakes are an important part of the learning process. You can't always get everything right at first go. Only if you lose the fear of making mistakes can you continue to improve. If your child is reluctant to try out an activity for fear of making a mistake, try to help them deal with it. Teach them to say: "Okay, I've made a mistake. I feel bad about it, but the best thing to do is learn from it. I should actually be grateful for making it – now I know how to do it and won't make the same mistake next time."

Jaromír Jágr is an immensely talented hockey player and has been the superstar of the NHL for years. To maintain this status, however, he needs to spend two hours in the gym every day. He probably has days when he hates it, but, at the age of 47, it's the only way to stay among the top players. (Jan: *I work out for an hour and a half every day, and sometimes I hate it, too!*) He keeps investing in his talent, and even though his professional hockey career is most likely nearing an end, it's incredible how long he's managed to stay among the elite. He might not be the fastest player on the ice anymore, but, after such a long career, he has an excellent feel for the game. His brain has myelinated certain connections and turned them into a habit, making Jaromír capable of performing well even under pressure. He's probably able to stay in flow for 90 percent of the game.

Having a talent for something doesn't automatically mean that you will be able to turn it into a career. Knowing your talents is not enough – you also need to put in a lot of effort and enthusiasm. Also, despite your talent for an activity, there might only be some specific things you actually like doing. Someone might be exceptionally musically gifted but they only like singing – they would never play an instrument. The only way to find out is to start developing the talent.

Jan: *My talents include strategic thinking, communication, and visionary skills. Some might think that would make me, for example, an excellent factory manager. I would hate that kind of job; it would stifle me. I hate repetitive work; I find it draining. I like working in business and marketing – fields that are constantly changing and moving forward. So why have I decided to lead workshops that focus on the same topics over and over again? Every workshop is different. Sometimes the participants are adults; sometimes I work with children, and every group is unique – just like my courses.*

Cyril Höschl: As a small boy, my son Cyril liked to make and build things; he had great manual and fine motor skills. As he grew up, he transformed this ability to manipulate the world with his hands into an ability to manipulate the world in his mind. He became a software engineer. Today, he's mostly too lazy to do manual work himself, but he's never lost the skills. The other day, he had workmen in his apartment to build some kind of partition. They kept telling him it wasn't possible to do it exactly the way he wanted to, so he bought a drill and fixed the partition himself – better than a professional joiner could have done. The only reason why he's never turned these skills into a career is that he finds creating software more challenging.

5

SELF-
CONFIDENCE

Self-confidence requires self-awareness: to believe in yourself, you first need to know yourself. It's important to understand your reactions under mental pressure because situations like that occur practically all the time: in school, at work, in sport, or in art. Add to this the stress of the ever-accelerating advancements in technology and you have your Monkey jumping all over the place, making it hard to focus. Self-awareness, together with discovering your talents, will help you achieve flow state more effectively and stay in it longer. Flow state allows you to deliver your best, which in turn allows you to believe in yourself much more.

Self-confidence is extremely important and closely depends on your strengths, talents, and genuineness. You can only be self-confident in those areas you are good at. You cannot trust yourself in areas you don't know anything about or which require skills you don't possess.

HOW TO BUILD UP YOUR CHILD'S SELF-CONFIDENCE

Building up self-confidence is essentially something everyone has to achieve on their own. Still, here are a few tips that could help you bolster your child's self-confidence.

- **Show your child that you love them.**

You know you love them to bits, but your child might see it differently. Assure them that you will still love them even when they mess up.

- **Do not make absolute judgments.**

Making absolute judgments will only undermine your child's self-confidence. Imagine your child getting annoyed while doing their home-work or drawing a picture. They might even tear the paper to pieces if the picture doesn't come out just right. You may lose your temper with them, but, even then, try to avoid needless absolute judgments: "You're so impatient! You simply can't concentrate. This happens all the time! You'll never do anything right." Or: "How many times have I told you not to spit out of the window? Only naughty, disgusting boys do that. You'll never grow up into a decent person!"

Corrective feedback is necessary, of course; you need to let your child know that certain behavior is simply not acceptable. However, giving feedback is not the same as losing your temper and calling your child stupid.

Here's what you could say: "I really don't like what you've done just now.

Tearing up your notebook? You can't do things like that." You should let the child feel they've done a bad thing, not that *they* are bad. Make them understand that criticizing them for something they've done is not the same as criticizing them as a person.

Perhaps you can recall a similar situation from your own childhood when your parents used to scold you endlessly and rehash your transgressions over and over again. Try to think about the person you are today. Have you really grown into an impatient woman or an insolent, naughty man? When you make a mistake, can you hear the little voice in the corner of your mind, telling you that you're an impossible klutz who simply can't do anything right? We often carry over these judgments to our adulthood, even though they may only be labels that got pinned on us when we were children.

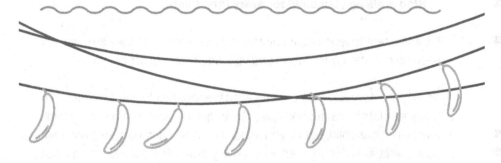

Making absolute judgments undermines a person's self-confidence. You should try to avoid them with your child as much as possible. Don't discuss the child's results but the activity itself – ask what they think they've done right, where they went wrong, and what they think they should improve.

- **Stop comparing your child to their siblings or other people's children.**

Parents tend to do this all the time – comparing their children to one another and comparing themselves to other people. Sometimes they are still being compared to others by *their* own parents, even though they're adults and have a family of their own. This kind of attitude is a residue of our own upbringing and education, as well as the influence of the general mindset within our society.

Try not to compare your child to anyone, either at home or in school/sports. Avoid saying things like: "How come Mary got an A on the test and you didn't?" "How come almost half the class got a better grade than you did?" "Your brother could do this just fine when he was your age!"

Simply stop comparing anyone. Your child, your partner, or yourself. Once you stop comparing yourself to others (friends, neighbors, coworkers), your life will be much easier. Try to help your child become the best they can be. If you think they're not trying hard enough, give them a gentle nudge. "You should go study some more. You can do much better than this."

- **Stop praising your child for every little thing.**

It's important to teach your child to be happy with who they are, without needing constant affirmation and validation from other people.

Some parents praise their child for even the slightest things. "You've eaten half your plate! What a good boy / clever girl you are!" You probably think this helps your child, but all you're doing is making communication with your child easier for yourself. Excessively praising a child for things that should be a matter of course (blowing their nose, tying up their shoes, eating their snack, saying "please" and "thank you", dressing on their own) will 1) make the child immune to such praise over time, and 2) make their own sense of self-worth dependent on other people's approval. And then, one day, a child shows their mother a picture they've painted, but she does not automatically praise them. The child is confused and disappointed. Are they not a "clever boy" or a "good girl" anymore? They may start pestering the parent until they get the validation they crave.

This does not mean you should stop praising your child altogether. Acknowledging the child has done well in certain situations is a good thing, but you should not go overboard. Try to focus your praise directly on the thing the child has accomplished.

Your child brings you a picture they've drawn. You could say: "Wow, you've drawn a new picture! What kind of crayons did you use? I like that you used so many different colors, even though it's only a little house. Do *you* like the picture? What do you like best about it?"

It's very important to ask your child whether they are actually happy with their work. You're teaching them not to wait for someone else's approval; instead, encourage them to assess their own work. A child that is happy with themselves feels more secure and stable, despite other people's reactions.

- **Take your child as seriously as you would like other people to take you.**

In the course of a single day, a child (especially at a very young age) will literally flood you with various ideas, stories, and theories. Most of them will not make any sense at all. You might be tempted to sigh: "How does he come up with all this rubbish? I wish he would clean up after himself instead of making up stupid stories."

Try to think about the reality filter that small children possess and how different it can be from ours. Is everything the child comes up with really rubbish, or are they just sharing the fruits of their vast imagination? Try to take your child seriously, even when they keep pestering you with the endless "why" questions. Once your child starts school, they will lose a huge chunk of the time they used to have for asking questions and sharing their ideas, and if you keep shooing them away at home, they will probably start being afraid to share their thoughts, ideas, and answers in class. They may think that their answers or opinions are not the "right" ones or that everyone will laugh at them if they say anything.

- **Listen to your child and try to understand their point of view.**

When setting rules and boundaries for your child, try to observe how the child reacts to them. Listen to your child. It can be pretty difficult sometimes, since children will explore various loopholes and make excuses to circumvent the rules you've set. Try to focus on the reasons they break the rules, and adjust the rules so that both you and your child can be happy with them. This means that once you set the boundaries and limits, your child can happily exist within those boundaries.

An adult's brain functions differently than a child's brain because it works on different wave frequencies (see the brainwave frequency table in Chapter 1). Sometimes the child simply does not want to listen and will do anything to disregard the rules. At other times, however, they may simply not understand what the parent is asking them to do, or they may be deeply immersed in flow state and can't "hear" what the parent is saying.

Try to remind yourself what you were like when you were little. Remember building a little village out of moss and twigs in the woods, populating it with pinecones as little wood elves? Remember how your mother told you to put on your sweatshirt and you didn't, too busy acting out a spectacular battle with your little forest pixies?

- **Respect your child's opinion, even if you disagree with it.**

When your child opposes you, don't take it as an act of defiance. The clash between the parent's and child's opinions may be quite difficult, especially in the case of older children whose personality is just starting to emerge.

You can influence your child's views to some extent, but there's no need for you to agree on everything. You can simply tell your child: "I don't like these torn blue jeans you're wearing, but I respect your taste…" "But you can't wear them to the theater," you may add.

- **Do not overload your child with instructions.**

We all know what it's like. You give your child one order after another, and then you get angry because they haven't managed to get even half of them done.

"Finish those mashed potatoes and drink your tea. Then brush your teeth, wash your face, and comb your hair. Pack your lunch box and get ready to go."

Your child does not yet have enough brain capacity to retain a long series of instructions and fulfill them one at a time until they're done. Their brain is not capable of such structured thinking. They try to follow the instructions, but while doing the first one, they forget the next. Try to give your child instructions one by one, and make sure they understand what you want from them. Explain yourself in a manner suitable for the child's age.

PARENTAL MISGIVINGS

Parents tend to have various concerns and misgivings regarding their parental role. However, instead of helping them to become better, more conscientious parents, such worries hinder them from enjoying the relationship with their children. "Am I a good enough parent?" "What if I am not doing everything I can for my child?" Even the most loving and caring parents can succumb to these doubts. Such misgivings, however, are entirely counterproductive and only undermine the parents' (and their children's) self-confidence.

Parents tend to project their fears onto their children, most likely copying their own parents' behavior. We all know these well-worn phrases:

"Don't stand so close to the water! You'll fall in."

"No, you can't play by the creek. You could drown."

"Don't swim too far! It's dangerous."

We often see parents hysterically keeping their baby away from a wading pool, in fear it might fall in. It's well known, however, that newborns are not afraid of water – it's their natural environment. Parents who keep their child away from the "dangerous" water will actually instill the fear of water in them. Soon they won't be able to get their toddler into a wading pool without a snorkel, inflatable armbands, and a swim ring. This may seem like an exaggeration to you, but it illustrates the way parents project their various fears onto their children (fear of water, heights, dogs, etc.).

Cyril Höschl: When our children were little, my wife used to spend a lot more time with them than I did. She was also the more anxious parent, always worrying that they would fall down, catch a cold, get injured... so I tried to balance it out and let them run free. I first took them rappelling when they were around five to seven years old. My daughter Kristina recently gave an interview about her hobby, mountain climbing. She said her love of climbing went all the way back to when she was a little girl, when I took her to the mountains and let her rappel down a rock. My other children took it as a great adventure, but that was it. For Kristina, the adrenaline rush she got from it resulted in a lifelong passion for climbing.

Try to think about all the fears you might be projecting onto your children every day and how many of them are actually justified.

Perhaps those warnings are something you used to hear from your parents, grandparents, or friends? Where do those fears stem from? Can you do something about them?

~~~~~~

Norwegian lecturer **Godi Keller** recalls his own experience with a child's fear of water. When he was little, his school stood near a river, and he and his friends used to play on the riverbank and swim in the stream. It was both a great adventure and a learning experience for them. There was one girl whose parents were environmental activists and made it their mission to fight for cleaner rivers – a commendable effort that unfortunately backfired. At home, all they talked about was pollution and poisonous substances in the water. The girl was so afraid to step in the water that she never joined her friends playing or swimming. Later in life, she turned her back on the environmentalist ideology altogether. Her parents had projected their own fear of contaminated water onto her and gave her no opportunity to have her own experiences and form her own judgment.

~~~~~~

Parents, grandparents, and most teachers are often convinced that whenever a child struggles with something, they need to correct them or, even better, show them how to do it right. This stems from the erroneous belief that children should master any skills as quickly and as well as possible but that they cannot do it without the help of an adult. (As if it was really necessary to do everything perfectly at the first try.) This might surprise you, but it's not always necessary to interfere with your child's efforts to learn a skill and try to show them how it's done. Some skills take the child a bit longer to learn and some come easily to them – but it's always better for the child to find out how to do things on their own. Learning through practice makes the knowledge/skill stick in the child's mind far better than being shown how to do it step by step. Trying out things on their own may take the child twice as long, but the Montessori "learning by doing" concept applies very much here.

Cyril Höschl: I think it was a good decision to let my children fend for themselves rather than always paving the way for them. I wouldn't change anything. "I'm not going to give you bread – I'm going to teach you how to bake it," is my motto. With young children, up until the age of 15, perhaps even 18, you obviously try to protect them against any unfair treatment, help them when they're in any kind of pain (whether emotional or physical), and care for them when they're ill. However, I am firmly against smoothing the way for them or giving them an unfair advantage. My daughter Karolina tried to get into medical school but failed the entrance exams. I was Dean of the Faculty of Medicine at the time, but I did not try to help her in any way.

The ubiquitous technology forces us to learn faster. Time-effectiveness is the key virtue of modern life. In view of this, parents may feel that it's important for their children to learn things as quickly and effectively as possible. The speed obsession is like a highly contagious disease. From the moment you get up, you start zooming around like a crazed bee: get dressed, eat your breakfast, brush your teeth, hop in the car, take the children to school, get to work. Your workload is enormous and your time is limited, so you deal with your tasks as soon as possible. As soon as you get off work, you need to rush to pick up the children, get the groceries, take the children to an after-school club, meet a friend...

When you get home, it's often quite late. You've barely stepped into your apartment, but you already have to start making dinner, get the children to do their homework, and then put them to bed. You have no patience for waiting around as a child tries things out. "You're so slow! Here, let me do it," you say frequently, not realizing that you're depriving your child of the chance to learn something on their own and undermining their mental resilience. You're paving their way, but you're not letting them choose their own path.

SOLUTION: FEEDBACK

The way you communicate with your child is extremely important. Making absolute judgments (you're impossible / incompetent / useless / stupid) means you're criticizing your child, not the particular thing they've done wrong. Instead of judging your child, try to provide them with useful feedback.

Judging someone means influencing their mental self-perception.

~~~~~~

You are in a hurry, waiting for your child to tie their shoes. "You're impossible! Six years old, and you still can't tie your shoes properly," you say impatiently. "We always have to wait for you." You're criticizing your child's inability to tie their shoes, but the child only hears the "You're impossible" part. Their Monkey starts spinning a negative mental story, and the child gradually starts applying their inability to tie their shoes to everything else. They start feeling useless, even though there are lots of other things they can do or learn faster than other kids their age. From thinking that they're useless because they can't meet their parents' expectations, they may start thinking they're useless in sports, as well as in school and basically everywhere else. Your casual remark started a negative downward spiral that could seriously damage your child's sense of self-worth. You should always be mindful of the way you communicate with your child.

~~~~~~

If you only give your child feedback about the specific thing they're doing wrong (or doing right), you're addressing that one particular issue. You're not judging your child.

You could say: "You know we're always in a hurry in the morning, and it still takes you far too long to tie your shoes. Here, let me help you now and look at what I'm doing. We're going to practice together tonight so you can do better next time. It's just a few simple moves; I'm sure you can do it."

If your child plays any sport (soccer, for example), you can ask them how they feel about the game they've just played: what they liked best, what they did well, and what they might want to improve before the next game. Do not simply ask about the score, or who won.

If all a parent cares about is their child's result, but has no interest in the way the child has achieved it, it might be difficult for them to learn the proper way to give feedback. When their child shows them a picture they've drawn at school, they will probably say something like: "Wow, that's beautiful! Did you get a good grade for it? Here, let's put it up on the fridge." They grab a magnet and stick the drawing on the refrigerator but show no further interest in it.

A parent who knows how to give proper feedback could say: "Here, show me. I like this picture a lot. Do *you* like it? What did you use to draw it? Was it hard to do? You can put it up somewhere if you want."

The first type of parent is (indirectly) telling their child that they only care about the result of their work (a good grade). The second parent, however, is expressing their interest in the child's work and offers them a chance to talk about it, reaffirming their affinity toward their favorite activity.

A child with the first type of parent may start being afraid of what might happen if they don't get a good grade, which stresses them out, stifles their creativity and willingness to compete and take risks, and slows down their learning process. Fear of a possible failure is extremely stressful.

A child with the second type of parent has the chance to explain their work to their parents, discuss it, and think about possible ways to improve in the future.

Why is that so important? You will find out in the next chapter.

BRINGING UP CHAMPIONS: INSPIRATION VS. MOTIVATION

Focusing on the **result** increases your motivation. People are usually motivated by external factors (good grades, gold medal, getting paid, getting a bonus), which means that by definition, motivation can only be short-term. It raises various logical questions: Under which conditions are you going to do the work? Who are you going to do it with? How much is it going to cost you? What do you have to do, and what will you get out of it? Logical questions are formed in the neocortex – the outermost layer of the brain, which is also the newest to evolve. It is not capable of creating deep emotional ties toward the subject/activity at hand, which means that motivation, though important, is not enough.

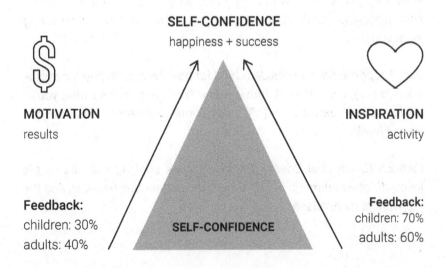

SELF-CONFIDENCE
happiness + success

MOTIVATION
results

INSPIRATION
activity

Feedback:
children: 30%
adults: 40%

SELF-CONFIDENCE

Feedback:
children: 70%
adults: 60%

Focusing on the **activity** itself gives you inspiration. The word "inspiration" comes from the Latin word "inspirare," which means "to breathe into" – so when you are inspired, you have an idea "blown into you." Inspiration lasts longer than motivation and provokes the following questions: How long have you been doing a certain activity? What method are you using to accomplish it, and how could you do it better next time? These questions stem from the right brain hemisphere, which is connected with emotions. Inspiration causes you to develop love for what you do: if you find something you have a natural aptitude for, you enjoy doing it. This creates a deep emotional tie to that particular activity, which may even become your life's mission.

If you only focus on the results (motivation), you are trying to win at any cost. This is where fear of failure kicks in, and suddenly you don't feel like competing at all.[18] If you are fixated on something, you are likely to fail: fear of possible failure prevents you from focusing on the present moment.

If you try to concentrate on the competition itself (activity / inspiration), you will finish the competition and fool your Monkey at the same time. Enjoyment trumps fixation every time.

The most successful athletes and businesspeople are those who love what they do. It rarely works the other way round: if you start doing something and decide to be the best, you will not suddenly start loving what you do.

Jan: *A reporter once asked Jaromír Jágr how he was finding the motivation to play, even after all those years. "You have no idea what you're talking about," Jaromír said. "It's not about motivation. It's about the love of hockey."*

Famous Czech chef Zdeněk Pohlreich loves cooking and shares his love with others through his TV shows, the restaurants he owns, and the cookbooks he publishes.

Bill Gates, my former boss, loved creating software. It was that love that made him the richest man in the world, not the other way around.

Results are important – but focusing solely on results triggers fear of failure.

Suggestion: When providing feedback to your child, devote only about 30 percent of it to the results of the child's activities (school grades, sports rankings, contests, etc.). The remaining 70 percent should be spent discussing the activity itself, regardless of the child's results (methods and techniques used, how the competition went, how the picture was painted, etc.).

This is the only way to raise champions. Children brought up with the right feedback from their parents become Olympic champions, successful artists, businesspeople, or professionals in any field they have a talent for (even a bricklayer can be a champion in their field, if they truly love what they do).

Martin Doktor is the best-known Czech sprint canoeist and double Olympic champion. When he was little, his father would only spend about 10 percent of the time discussing his results and 90 percent on feedback about the race itself.

David Svoboda is a Czech athlete who competes in the modern pentathlon. When he lost a competition as a child, his mother would tell him: "You didn't do so good because you have something much better ahead of you."

Olympic champions and successful people in general spend only about 30 percent of their time analyzing their results but spend the rest of their time focusing on their sport/profession instead.

If you focus on discussing the method your child has achieved a certain result with, rather than the result itself, your child will be able to realize that their favorite activity is a series of unique present moments – one after another. If a child has an aptitude for a certain activity, you need to help them get into a flow state as much as possible, instead of focusing on the end result. They will still work under pressure, but the pressure is going to encourage their creativity (flow state causes us to stop taking notice of time, turn off our inner critic, and utilize our talents to the maximum). You can only get into flow state if you are fully immersed in the present moment. Discussing an activity step by step helps your child understand that if you play tennis, you play one ball at a time; you fill out test questions one at a time; and you live your life one moment at a time.

Children are very perceptive and can sense if their parents only care about their results. To prove themselves, they tend to get fixated on the results as well. Feedback centered around results does not help the child to improve and develop – instead, it increases their fear of possible failure. The child's subconscious starts telling them that it doesn't matter *how* they achieve a result – as long as they do. The subconscious need to succeed might even lead to cheating.

Focusing solely on results does not allow your child to improve. Only if you focus on the activity itself can you help your child to make progress.

IDEAL FEEDBACK METHOD

For children, the ideal proportion of result-oriented and activity-oriented feedback is 30:70. For adults, it is about 40:60.

When giving feedback, it is important for the parent/coach to deliver criticism in such a way that the child stays inspired and keeps their enjoyment of the activity at hand. Feedback involving absolute judgments, or including only those things the child has done wrong, could cut the emotional connection and put them off the activity for good. That's why we recommend using what's known as the **feedback sandwich method**.

FEEDBACK SANDWICH

- First, tell your child what they have done right. Show them your approval. This produces positive emotions that flood the child's brain with the hormone serotonin, which works as a buffer against the corrective feedback that is to follow.

- Now comes the time for corrective feedback. Discuss what the child has done wrong. The criticism should always concern the activity itself, not your child as a person. Do not undermine your child's self-confidence by making absolute judgments.

- In the last phase of the feedback sandwich, express your trust in the future. You could say, for example: "It would be great if you could learn from the mistakes you've made. You're good at this. We believe in you." Showing confidence in your child is extremely important. It causes your child's brain to produce oxytocin, also known as the hormone of love and trust. Bolster this by making physical contact with your child: stroke their hair or pat them on the shoulder.

> Feedback delivered by the sandwich method will ensure that the child does not lose the emotional connection with the activity at hand, which could happen if the parents only focus on the child's results.

Parents often put pressure on their child: "You have to get good grades." "You have to be the best." "You have to do this." "You have to do that." The child soon realizes that good results are the only thing their parents care about and starts being afraid of failure. Long-term success in any career requires a healthy, reasonable attitude toward both achievements and failures. If you manage to learn from your mistakes, you can return to the present (mistakes are a thing of the past and you can't do anything to change them), which in turn allows you to shape your future.

Parents should not focus solely on the child's results. If they stick to the 30:70 feedback sandwich rule (30 percent results, 70 percent activity), they reassure their child that, instead of getting results, they want the child to improve and make progress in their favorite activity.

Jan: *At tennis tournaments, I often see parents – usually dads – yelling at their children and calling them names. Those parents have never achieved anything in life and now live vicariously through their children. It's only a matter of time until the children quit playing altogether because there is no enjoyment in it for them anymore and they are afraid to lose. Some may even grow to hate the game they used to excel at.*

Kateřina: *We once had an 11-year-old boy at one of our workshops who played the violin beautifully but was afraid to perform before an audience – not because of his parents, but because of the strangers among the spectators. He would play easily and with enthusiasm at home, but as soon as he stepped on the stage, he felt terribly scared.*

"Do you like playing the violin?" we asked him. "How much do you like it?" – "I love it," he said.

"Then you need to think about it this way," we told him. "'I love play-ing the violin. When I play, I play one note at a time. It doesn't matter whether there's ten people watching me or 10,000. I play because I like playing.' Those people have come to listen to you. If you think too much about the audience, you become afraid of making a mistake and getting no applause. You're afraid of failure. It's the Monkey in your head, doing what we call 'emotional hijack.' It disturbs you from the flow state and the present moment. Try to focus on playing one note at a time. Remember how much you love playing. You just need to make the switch in your head."

Dagmar Svobodová has brought up three sons: David, Tomáš, and Pavel. All of them are very successful in what they do, and they do what they enjoy. One of them, David Svoboda, is an Olympic cham-pion in the modern pentathlon, and one of our close collaborators.

When raising her children, Dagmar always relied on her common sense and intuition. She has shared with us some of her most impor-tant parenting principles, firmly convinced that it is those principles that helped her sons to achieve success. As the mother of three ener-getic, active boys, she had to discover activities they would enjoy and stick with them.

Here are some of her parenting tips:

- Observe your children closely to find out what they like doing.
- Treat all your children fairly; don't play favorites.
- Encourage your children to work as a team.
- With enough determination, anything is possible.
- Every child is different and should be treated as a unique individual.
- **It's far more important to find an activity that your children will enjoy, rather than focusing on their performance and results.**

MENTAL RESILIENCE

Mental resilience is the ability to control your thoughts and emotions in order to achieve the best results, even under difficult and strenuous conditions. In today's society, which exerts enormous pressure on the individual, this skill is of primary importance.

Almost since birth, people labor under the assumption that it's our thoughts that make us who we are. Identifying with one's thoughts, however, leads to difficulties. Approximately 60,000 thoughts run through our brain on any single day, and 98 percent of those are highly repetitive. It helps to realize that even though you have so many thoughts, you don't necessarily need to identify them; instead, you can watch them as if from a slight distance, like an impartial observer. This will allow you to recognize negative thoughts and nip them in the bud. You may realize that what has set off the negative thought was a trivial thing that does not deserve your attention.

The more you learn to view your thoughts like an impartial observer, the more control you will have over them. Consequently, you will also be able to control the emotions related to those thoughts. If you simply let a thought run through your mind, nothing will happen. As soon as you start dissecting it or rating it (positive vs. negative emotion), you step out of flow. Losing a tennis match, for example, does not necessarily have to be caused by a negative emotion, like fear of failure. Even a positive emotion can have a negative impact on your performance. When you're doing particularly well, you may start looking forward to winning the match, which throws you out of the flow state, and you end up losing. You need to play one ball at a time and stay in the present moment the whole game.

Mental resilience allows you to stay focused and not succumb to either negative or positive thoughts and emotions. Which is exactly what you need.

MARSHMALLOW TEST

The so-called Stanford marshmallow experiment[19] was a series of studies on delayed gratification, led by psychologist Walter Mischel at Stanford University, California, some 40 years ago. Preschool-aged children were led to a room and offered a choice: they could either take one small reward (a marshmallow), or if they waited a little more, usually 15 to 20 minutes, they would get two rewards. After that, the tester left the room and left the children to their own devices. Only about a third of the participants waited long enough to earn the extra marshmallow; the rest of the children ate the one marshmallow before the set time limit.

The researchers followed the children's progress over the subsequent 30 years, with the following results: those who were able to wait longer for the bigger reward (in other words, those who were more mentally resilient, since waiting was mentally draining on such small children), tended to have better school results and life outcomes than those who preferred to be given a smaller reward without having to wait.

The experiment proved that mentally resilient individuals tend to be significantly more competent than those who prefer instant gratification. It illustrated the importance of mental resilience and proved that paving a child's way in life was counterproductive. It's far better to let children face difficult situations and/or decisions, even at an early age. Children who are used to having their path smoothed for them tend to give up at the first sign of possible failure. Mentally resilient children, on the other hand, take self-doubt in their stride.

Bill Gates: Every NO gets you closer to a YES.

Mental resilience means not accepting a NO as a final answer. Instead, you should make an effort to turn it into a YES. This is the mindset you need to make progress. Children's mental resilience is determined by their parents to a considerable extent. If a parent does not allow the child to make mistakes and/or accept that making mistakes is natural, their child will not gain enough mental resilience to avoid constant fear of failure.

Jan: *I used to play tennis as a child. It was great training for my future corporate career. I used to play with Ivan Lendl; he was only two years older than me. While most of the junior players worked almost exclusively on their physical fitness, Ivan would focus on mental training and conditioning. He had this little ritual – before each serve, he would brush clay off his shoes. He did it even when there was no clay. It gave him an extra two seconds to calm down. He had an extremely hard and fast serve, so those two seconds were quite unsettling for his opponents, who must have been thinking: "What's he doing? He should be serving, and he's cleaning his shoes!" It was this little ritual that prevented Ivan's Monkey from stirring up doubts about the serve's outcome. He was fully immersed in the present moment, and the Monkey had no chance.*

Kateřina: *I used to play basketball for many years when I was little. It was great training in mental resilience. I was about ten years old when the coach made us run lap after lap because he wanted even the slowest girls to catch up with the fastest. After a few laps, most girls were in tears. As the team captain, I decided we would show him! My friend and I grabbed the slowest girls by the hand and literally dragged them to the finish line. It wasn't easy dragging mostly overweight girls (forced to play the sport by their parents in order to get some exercise, not because they really wanted to play basketball) and trying to look cheerful and encouraging – but we did it.*

Mental resilience is the ability to control one's thoughts in a difficult situation and prevent your inner Monkey from warning against making a mistake.

If you make a mistake, you have two options:

Break down and fail / lose.

Tell yourself that a mistake is really a path toward doing something better next time: learn from it, return to the present moment, and continue as before.

~~~~~~

Soccer player Petr Čech: No matter what the score is, I always play like it is still nil-nil.

~~~~~~

Cristiano Ronaldo has played soccer since he was only about three years old. His successful soccer career clearly illustrates how important it is to start training your brain at an early age. Ronaldo volunteered as a test subject in a study conducted by a modern research lab. He and another player were locked up in a room and asked to play.

Ronaldo's teammate had to pass the ball to him, and Ronaldo was then supposed to head-butt the ball and try to score a goal. As soon as the first player touched the ball, the lights in the lab went out. Ronaldo had to head the ball in total darkness. He was given ten attempts – and succeeded each and every time. How is that possible?

Ronaldo's subconscious is like a computer, calculating all the possible outcomes of a player coming into contact with the ball. He always knows where a ball will land and what spin it's going to have. This allows him to score more goals than most players. He's been perfecting this skill since he was a little boy, so it's become automated. Everything he does, he's done countless times before. He's capable of staying in flow for 90 percent of the game time.[20]

~~~~~~

Mental resilience is not taught in schools. It can't be learned – you have to build it up. It is healthy and beneficial to improve both physical and mental fitness. Resilience can only be built up through ample practice.[21] This goes for both parents and children.

Jan: *As a boy, one of the things that helped me build up my mental resilience was having to get up early on weekends. Since the age of 12, I had to get up at 4am for an early morning training session. Today, however, I don't have a problem getting up at 5am on a Saturday and going jogging, while some people can barely make it to the office around 9am. To be able to get up so early, I had to turn the practice into a habit.*

[15] Source: Gallup. Available at http://news.gallup.com/poll/165269/worldwide-employees-engaged-work.aspx

[16] Source: Ready to Manage. Available at http://blog.readytomanage.com/coaching-models-johari-window/

[17] Source: Jan Mühlfeit, Melina Costi (2016). *The Positive Leader*. FT Press.

[18] Many children who score as "competitive" in our tests don't actually want to compete at all, so afraid are they of losing.

[19] Source: Walter Mischel (2014). *The Marshmallow Test: Mastering Self-control*. Little, Brown and Co.

[20] The test results, as well as commentaries of prominent soccer experts, are presented in a documentary titled *Ronaldo Tested to the Limit*.

[21] Every individual is different and unique in their initial level of endurance (usually depending on the conditions they grew up in).

6

SELF-WORTH

FREEDOM TO CHOOSE

"Freedom to choose" is a concept that was first coined by Austrian neurologist and psychiatrist Viktor Frankl. Born into a Jewish family, Frankl was a survivor of several Nazi concentration camps; the probability of such survival was only 1:28.

Frankl claimed that while we cannot influence the circumstances in our lives, we can choose the way we respond to those circumstances: we are free to choose our attitude. An individual is not defined by what is happening to them and around them but by their own actions and decisions.[22] This principle has been verified by scientific research.

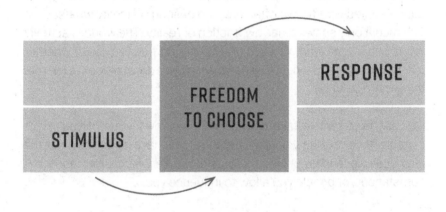

Apart from genetic predisposition, an individual's way of thinking is greatly influenced by their outside circumstances (where they live, what they see and hear, etc.), as well as by the internal dialogue that is happening inside their mind (sometimes also known as self-talk). Through self-talk, an individual makes up internal mental stories that become imprinted on their subconscious. The human subconscious is like a garden: the kind of fruit it bears depends on the seeds you plant in it. If you deliberately fashion your inner dialogue to form a positive opinion of yourself, you load up your subconscious with positive data. Negative thoughts and mental stories, on the other hand, are like weeds: sooner or later they will infest and smother your mental garden.

Jan: *I tried to join a tennis club when I was little. The first time I came to practice, the coach said to me: "You're too fat. You should try sumo wrestling." I had two choices: I could either try sumo, or I could stop overeating and start exercising. I chose the second option. Within a year, I was the best junior player in the club, and I beat the coach's own son in a match. Not only did I become a better athlete, I also improved my mental resilience.*

Always form your own opinions, regardless of what others try to tell you. People around us, politicians, the media – they all try to sell us their opinions. It's important to choose which information you listen to and allow to influence you. If you choose to watch tragic news reports and gory movies all the time, your opinion of the world will likely be pretty dark. People's worldviews often have no bearing on reality whatsoever. The media only shows a narrow fraction of reality. The world is actually much better than what you see on TV. You are free to choose whether to let the ever-present negative news weigh you down or look for something more uplifting.

It's very important to take control over your own mind. If you're not capable of controlling your own thoughts, you have no control over the filter you use to interact with the outside world: which information, circumstances, or people you allow to influence you.

EXERCISE: FREEDOM TO CHOOSE

Write down the following formula: $S + R = O$

Explain to your child that S means "situations" – everything that happens in your life. "R" means "response" – your reaction to those situations. "O" stands for "outcomes" – what you feel as a consequence of the situations in your life and your responses to them. Almost every day, you meet people who are deeply unhappy with the "outcomes" in their life: they feel lonely, miserable, or angry; they are not doing well in school or in sports; their parents are being mean to them; and so on. Those outcomes, however, depend on the way you respond to various situations in your life.

A student who is new in class may perceive their new schoolmates as weird or hostile and will feel very lonely. However, they could choose to introduce themselves with a smile and try to strike up new friendships as soon as possible. The situation remains the same (new student in class), but the outcome will be dramatically different.

Try to act out some of the following situations with your child, using different responses each time, and observe the outcomes.

Situation (S):

A teacher punishes a student unjustly.
Ask someone to help you get a baby carriage into a tram or a bus.
Ask someone to watch your dog while you do your shopping.
You are collecting money for a high school graduation party.
You need to ask someone to lend you their bike.

Types of responses (R) you can use:

diffident, humble behavior
friendly request
overbearing, bossy attitude
shy or aloof behavior
giving an order

The outcome (O) – other people's behavior toward you – depends on every person involved in the interaction.

Finally, discuss the exercise with your child. Note which ways led to the best outcomes and whether the response chosen played an important part or not.

MAJOR LEAGUE THINKING

You are the CEO of your own mind.

No one can tell you what to think. Inside your mind, you have absolute freedom: freedom to choose what to think. Your mind is your strongest weapon. To be able to wield it, however, you need good training.

Whenever you have a negative thought (which reflects immediately on your physical well-being: negative thoughts generate negative emotions, which drain you of physical energy), it is possible to stop that thought and trace it back to its origins. Negative thoughts are often caused by the most trivial of things, which is closely related to a too-narrow reality filter.

Excellent athletes or artists have negative thoughts like everyone else, but they are able to stave off their negative response to them.

At any given second, we are surrounded by some 11 million bits of information. The human brain, however, is only capable of processing 120 bytes of information per second. This means that our reality filter is extremely narrow. The way you think about yourself shapes both your reality filter and, as a consequence, your entire life. Every thought that runs through your brain generates certain chemicals. Depending on the way your brain synapses connect, this has either a beneficial or detrimental effect on your psyche.

Your filter, for example, can be solely focus-oriented, which makes you afraid of failure. If you feel, on the other hand, that the activity itself is far more important than the results, your reality filter serves as a means of inspiration, which helps you achieve flow state far more often.

Jan has decided to call this principle **Major League Thinking**. If you were brought up to think that you can be a "major league player" in a certain field, preferably one for which you have a talent, you will indeed become one. After a mistake, you may occasionally drop to the minor league, but your mental resilience and your sense of self-worth can pull you back up.

If you were brought up to think you couldn't ever do better than division level, you will never make it out of your local club.

It doesn't matter whether you grew up in a small town with few opportunities or in a large city.

Jan: *I grew up in a tiny village in the Bohemian-Moravian Highlands. I lived there until I was 19.*

It doesn't even matter how much education you get.

Jan: *I nearly didn't finish college.*

Or what your first job is.

Jan: *I used to work as a night watchman.*

What **does** matter is your ability to imagine that you can become a major league player, even if only once. If you can't, then you never will.

Jan: *I was once granted an audience by Prince Charles to discuss university education with him. If I'd let it get to me that I was just an ordinary boy from a Czech village, going to talk to a prince, I would have run before I even made it into the room.*

"Major league" may mean something different for everyone, in any activity and profession. You can be a bricklayer and still be major league – superb masons are masters in their craft, towering over their colleagues, just like in any other profession. Even a bricklayer can work in a state of flow.

Jan: *I once asked David Svoboda how he came to win the Olympic gold. "Because I worked my butt off," he said. "And I had the best conditions. My mom brought up all of us children to be winners. Whenever my brothers or I messed up, she would tell us it didn't matter, that there was something better waiting for us out there." This attitude toward making mistakes is very uncommon among parents.*

The concept of Major League Thinking is further supported by theories coined by Bruce H. Lipton in his book *The Biology of Belief* (Hay House, 2008). Lipton claims that every thought we allow to enter our subconscious produces certain chemicals in the brain which can affect a person's success and happiness in life.

Self-confident people who do what they enjoy and what they have an aptitude for are able to get into flow very often. This causes their brain to produce serotonin and oxytocin – both are hormones capable of inducing a state of happiness and euphoria. By contrast, those who do things they do not enjoy or are not competent in get into a constant state of stress. Stress causes the brain to produce cortisol and adrenaline – hormones which induce a state of fear, increase our heart rate, and cause shallow breathing and trepidation. All of this can ultimately lead to depression or burnout. This is something you should watch out for. You may be convinced you're not mentally resilient and that you are prone to depression when in fact you have been moving toward it for a long time.

Anyone can master Major League Thinking.

Suggestion: Be more of who you are. Be yourself. Do what you have a talent for, and be genuine. You don't need to imitate anyone.

You can think of your Monkey (the amygdala) as your ego: constantly whispering in your ear and telling you how to behave so that people see you the way you want. Your ego, however, is not really *you*. Think of it as a "user interface." People who are truly successful are usually very genuine. They have no need to pretend or imitate anyone, and they certainly do not have an overinflated ego. Bill Gates is a very normal guy. So was Steve Jobs.

VISIONS AND VISUALIZATION

Anything a human mind can imagine can be done.

Children would have a hard time grasping the things we have discussed here. Freedom to choose, Major League Thinking, the inner workings of our brain... those are difficult concepts to fully comprehend, even for an adult. Explaining these complex concepts to children can be done through visualization exercises. Show your children that their mind is closely interconnected with their body. Whenever they imagine something (a dream or a future goal) and try to actually see it in their mind (you can encourage them to do it with their eyes closed), they are actually "fooling" their body, in a good way, into believing that what they have visualized has actually occurred. Their conviction that whatever they've imagined may come true can affect both themselves and their outside circumstances.

The following exercise works for both adults and children. Try it out and see how closely your mind and body are connected.

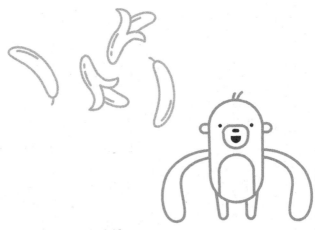

142

EXERCISE: VISUALIZATION

1. Stand up straight. Do not move – keep your feet firmly attached to the ground. Stretch your right arm forward and focus on it. Imagine that you have a camera in your mind. It's recording everything you see around you. Look at your outstretched hand, in the direction your fingertips are pointing. Slowly, start spinning your arm around, keeping it outstretched. Watch everything around you. Spin your arm clockwise until it becomes slightly uncomfortable. When you feel like you've stretched your arm to the limit, and your body won't let you move it any further, stop and try to commit to memory where your fingers are pointing. Imagine pushing a pin into that exact spot. Look a little bit further, beyond your hand. Take in everything around you and record it with your inner camera.

   We always tell children to imagine that their feet are glued to the ground to prevent them from shifting their weight from one foot to the other or running around.

   This is a great visualization exercise that allows children to calm down and take in everything around them – even the silence, which is normally nearly impossible.

2. Now close your eyes. Imagine your feet are still firmly attached to the ground, your arms hanging loosely by your sides. Go inside your head and the camera you've created there.

   Your hand will be pointing somewhere into the distance – to the wall, a poster, or anything else in the room.

3. Imagine your right arm rising, but without actually doing it. Imagine looking at it and then replay the rotating movement you did while "recording." With your eyes closed, watch your hand spinning slowly around, taking in the entire room like you did before. Keep going slowly until you

get to the point where you've put your "pin." Stop and tell yourself: "Now I'm looking at the spot where my pin is." However, since everything is now going on inside your head without being limited by your body, you can imagine rotating the whole 360 degrees round your own axis. Imagine your waist twisting as if you're trying to wring out a wet cloth. Once you've turned the whole 360 degrees, start spinning back. Imagine your outstretched arm unwinding again. Stop for a second at the spot where your "pin" is, and slowly get back to the starting position. You can open your eyes now. If there was something missing or something you couldn't imagine quite right, take a quick peek around to complete the picture. Now try rotating around in your mind again. Now that you've done it once before and are much more comfortable with the exercise, it will work even better. Close your eyes and take a spin around the spot where you've put your pin, at your own pace – until you're all twisted, like a cloth being wrung out. Then untwist again.

4. For the last part of the exercise, keep your eyes open. Step out of your head and focus back on your body, still firmly glued to the ground. Stretch your right arm forward and repeat the exercise you did at the beginning. Rotate your arm as far as your body will let you. If you focused enough with your eyes closed, your body should now let you get a little bit further than the spot you previously pushed your "pin" into.

Children tend to enjoy this visualization exercise: most of them will manage to make their body stretch beyond its initial limits and realize that it really works. They usually want to try again and again, showing the exercise to their parents or other kids. Once you make your mind believe you can do something, you can trick your body into complying. The rotating arm is quite a trivial exercise. However, once you imagine any particular dream or goal and make yourself believe you can actually achieve it, you can fool your body into actually cooperating with you – which puts you one step closer to that dream or goal. Visualizations offer a significant mental boost.

The concept also works the other way round – you can make your mind follow your body. If you become beset by negative thoughts and a fear of failure, strike a self-confident, victorious pose, your entire body exuding an "I can do this!" attitude. Your posture will influence the way you think.

WHY VISIONS WORK

Visions can be defined as an imagined world – an idea of something which does not yet exist but which we believe in. Without visions, there would be no progress – every new invention or idea first comes into existence inside the human mind. Only then can it also start existing in physical reality, by getting accomplished or manufactured.

Kateřina: *It's good to share your visions with others and possibly also inspire them. Had I not been regaling Jan with my enthusiastic rants about having worked with children and how much I would like to do it again, our "Unlocking a Child's Potential" project would perhaps never have come into existence. Jan saw my determination and enthusiasm and came up with the idea to connect our two worlds – his many years of global experience in coaching, personal development, and positive leadership and my specialization in new education methods for children.*

HOW VISIONS ARE FORMED

Our subconscious mind works like a computer. It makes connections and collects data extremely fast, regardless of whether the data we feed it is real or not. The more we imagine something happening, the more we increase the probability that it actually *will* happen. Once we visualize something, we start believing it.

~~~~~~~~~~~~~~~~~~~~~~~~~~

When **Bill Gates** started his business, all he had was his love for designing software and a vision of a personal computer in every home. At that time, the smallest computer took up a whole room, and people mocked Gates for his ideas; 11 years later, he was the richest man in the world. How was that possible? When a visionary manages to persuade people to believe in their idea, they follow his or her lead. Visions are groundbreaking thoughts that often have the potential to change the world.

~~~~~~~~~~~~~~~~~~~~~~~~~~

Mahatma Gandhi had no army or any real power to influence events. All he had was a vision of India's liberation from the British Empire. Once the people of India embraced his vision, they managed to make it come true.

~~~~~~~~~~~~~~~~~~~~~~~~~~

Had **Martin Luther King's** famous speech begun with the words: "I have a plan...," no one would have believed in him. He chose a much more powerful phrase: "I have a dream." A dream is a vision fueled by emotion. King dreamed of black and white children going to school hand in hand; 230,000 people gathered to listen to King's speech – an amazing turnout for a time when no social media existed. They came because they believed in his vision, and more than one third of them were white people, who were just as sick of racial segregation as he was.

~~~~~~~~~~~~~~~~~~~~~~~~~~

Henry Ford was a very talented engineer. Designing and manufacturing cars, however, required a lot of research and experimentation – and many blunders.

~~~~~~~~~~~~~~~~~~~~~~~~~~

It was not just an amazing talent that made **Thomas Edison** America's greatest inventor. His discoveries required thousands of experiments and decades of research – but his visions were clear from the start.

Visions are at the start of each invention, victory, change, or success. The better you are able to visualize things, the more you increase the probability of them actually happening.

Turning your inborn talents into strengths requires effort: not only real, practical training and improvement of your talents but also strengthening your power of visualization and learning to analyze your talents and the progress you've made.

Imagine you have a tremendous talent for decathlon. All you want is the Olympic gold. Becoming an Olympic champion requires immense effort – which also includes the power to imagine yourself in the moment of victory. If you are unable to visualize your success, it will never happen.

Jan: *When coaching athletes, newly appointed managers, or CEOs, I like to use a visualization technique I learned from a certain mental coach in the US. It involves looking at your journey toward success from a point in the future, which can offer valuable insight into the present.*

I worked with Czech track cyclist Tomáš Bábek. In the spring of 2010, he was hit by a car and went into a coma. Doctors gave him a very slim chance of survival and going back to cycling seemed out of the question. But Tomáš surprised everyone. He went on to win the 2016 European Championships and came back second in the 2017 World Championships.

I gave him an exercise called "Letter to Younger Self" to work on. "Imagine winning the Tokyo Olympics in 2020," I told him. "And then imagine your future self writing a letter to your present self, who is training for the games. Tell him what happened over those two years." He thought about it for a moment and then described everything that would have happened. "Fine, and now imagine yourself standing on the podium. You've won, they're playing the Czech anthem, the flag is rising..." I wanted him to tell me how he felt. "I can't," he said. "I'm just completely immersed in what's going on."

EXERCISE: A LETTER TO YOUR YOUNGER SELF

Together with your child, set up a time frame within which they would like to achieve a certain goal.

Example: 12-year-old George would like to get into a high school of his choice in three years. He's a big IT fan and wants to get into a high school that offers a specialization in information technology.

Now guide your child through the exercise.

Imagine you're 15 and you've actually been accepted to the school you wanted. Now you're writing a letter to the 12-year-old George. Tell him what he needs to do to make his dream come true. Describe in detail everything you had to go through and accomplish. Take a look back from that best possible future and set out some milestones along the way.

The more detailed the letter, the better – often it's only in hindsight that you realize what steps you had to take to achieve your goal. George needs to improve his grade in math and learn a lot more about hardware (he doesn't like it as much as writing code, but he will need it to get into an IT-focused school).

The letter looks back at the present from the best possible future and should define certain milestones that are required to achieve the desired goal. There are two types of milestones:

Result-oriented. What do you need to accomplish to achieve your goal? (Example: Athletes need to fulfill qualification requirements. George needs to improve his math grade.)

We explained in earlier chapters what myelination means: strengthening brain synapses through regular repetition of a certain activity. If you want to master a sport, you need to practice it regularly. That is, however, only the first step toward success. Apart from physical training, you also need to think about the sport so that your mind receives the appropriate stimuli along with your body. Last but not least, you need to imagine your future success. Research has proven that visualizing an activity has nearly the same effect on myelin production as the activity itself.

Suggestion: Let's say you are a professional tennis player who has been injured and has to skip training for a while. It is good to keep practicing mentally, even lying in a hospital bed after surgery. It still counts.

It is important to have faith. Both your personality and outward reality are shaped by what you believe.[23]

Some people may think of themselves as "visionaries." It's not enough, however, to have a vision: you need to believe in that vision wholeheartedly – and if the vision is to change the world, then the people following you need to believe in it as much as you do. The greatest leaders, innovators, and reformers in history were those who were able to share their vision of the future and communicate it in a way that made others believe in it.

Had Thomas Edison brooded over his every failure, he would have never accomplished any of his visions. Instead, he viewed each of his failed experiments as a result in itself and learned from his mistakes. He wrote them off as a path that did not lead to his goal and started again. He loved what he did and always focused on the present moment. He loved inventing, not his inventions.

Everyone can ask themselves: Do I like victory, or do I like winning?

If the only thing you care about is victory itself, you will never achieve as much as when you enjoy the actual process of winning. You can find out more about activity and results in Chapter 5.

You can only fulfill your visions if you are able to work in flow state. It is much easier to get into flow if you love what you do and if you can support your effort through visualization. Flow state allows you to deliver an optimal performance and increases your creativity. You cannot create and invent under stress; the best innovations are always produced in flow state. Groundbreaking ideas require a relaxed state of mind where you lose track of time. Acute awareness of the passage of time induces stress and activates your Monkey.

Flow state can also be achieved through meditation. When you medi-tate, your brain operates on the same brainwave frequency as during flow (alpha, which is 8–12 Hertz, or theta, which is 4–8 Hertz – more details in the brainwave frequency chart in Chapter 1). Meditation also boosts creativity. When you're under stress, your brain cannot access information in your subconscious. As soon as you manage to achieve either alpha or theta level, your mind calms down, and you will be able to both pull information from your subconscious and store it in there, which is essential for the creative process. Visualization also works far better in this state.

You can read more on meditation and other techniques of training your Monkey in Chapter 7.

Visualization requires you to connect with your subconscious, which stores an enormous amount of information (everything you have ever learned, for example). On the alpha frequency level, you can also imagine your future. You can do that easily because your inner critic is currently turned off. (If your Monkey were awake, it would most likely interfere by putting doubts in your mind.)

The more often you visualize your future, the more you start believing in it. It really works – just look at some of the world's best athletes.

HAPPINESS

The feeling of happiness is caused by four chemical substances produced by our brain. The brain also produces those substances in flow state. (It's therefore a logical assumption that our sense of happiness is closely related to our need for self-fulfillment: the more time we spend in flow state, the happier we are.)

FOUR CHEMICALS THAT INDUCE HAPPINESS

The first two happiness-inducing hormones, endorphin and dopamine, can be produced by the brain even if a person is alone.

ENDORPHIN-fueled happiness is triggered by physical exertion. Endorphins prevent you from feeling fatigue and pain, so if you are doing something you truly enjoy, a flow state allows you to work or train longer. It's the reason why a child will not fall asleep when playing, even if they are extremely tired. Take, for example, Roger Federer, the oldest tennis player (40) who has managed to retain his number-one rank for many consecutive years. Federer is able to play in flow for 90 percent of the game. The endorphins his brain releases allow him to beat even much younger opponents.

DOPAMINE is also known as the "finish line chemical." Its production is triggered as a last reserve when you are close to getting a reward.

A good example is a child working on a math test. They don't have much time left, but they still have several problems to solve. The child's brain produces dopamine, which provides a burst of energy necessary to work faster and finish on time.

Emil Zátopek, the famous Czech athlete of the postwar era, used to say: "When you feel like you can't run anymore, run faster." Many people thought he was exaggerating, but he was right. Flow state was an unknown concept then, but Zátopek knew instinctively that the human body was capable of a short spurt just before the finish line.

The other two "happiness hormones," serotonin and oxytocin, can only be produced in the company of other people.

SEROTONIN is produced when you feel important and rewarded. A good example is a child playing an instrument in front of an audience. The more they enjoy playing and the more appreciation they sense from the listeners, the stronger their flow state. This triggers the production of serotonin and the subsequent feeling of happiness.

OXYTOCIN is also known as the "hormone of love and trust." Its production is stimulated when you are in the company of someone you can trust or who can trust you.

WHAT IS HAPPINESS?

Happiness means something a little different for everyone. Some people are convinced they have control over their own happiness. Others claim that happiness is something we cannot influence in any way or even claim that happiness is genetically determined.

Sonja Lyubomirsky is a professor in the Department of Psychology at the University of California, Riverside, and author of the book *The How of Happiness: A Scientific Approach to Getting the Life You Want.*

Lyubomirsky specializes in positive psychology and the study of happiness. Based on her team's many years of research, she has created a chart illustrating what actually determines a person's sense of happiness.

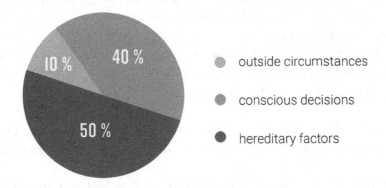

- outside circumstances
- conscious decisions
- hereditary factors

THREE FACTORS DETERMINING HAPPINESS

HEREDITARY FACTORS – this includes genetic predispositions inherited from one's parents and ancestors. Until recently, scientists were convinced that there is no way to change or influence our genetic predispositions; however, the results of the latest research conducted by geneticists and psychologists indicate that this is not completely true.

Everyone is born with certain talents and weaknesses. Success, however, is always achieved through what you *can* do, not through that which you are not particularly good at.

Jan: *I can't think of a single person who has achieved success through their weaknesses.*

Genetics constitutes approximately 50 percent of the factors influencing your happiness, which is quite a lot. You can't swap the cards nature has dealt you, but you can decide which cards to play and which to hold back or even discard altogether. No one is born completely happy or unhappy; your own attitude toward happiness can do a great deal.

OUTSIDE CIRCUMSTANCES – those are the conditions you exist in: the place where you live, your current situation in life, the work you do, your physical health, your family and loved ones, etc. To a certain extent, you can have control over some of those circumstances (by choosing a profession or a place to live, for example). However, everyone has a different starting line, and some people have more control over their own life than others. Even though many people are mistakenly convinced that outside circumstances play a crucial role, they make up only 10 percent of the factors influencing our happiness.

CONSCIOUS DECISIONS – those are factors that you have complete control over, such as your attitude toward a certain situation or your past.

Whenever something happens to you, good or bad, you are free to decide how you are going to handle it. You can learn from your mistakes and move on, stronger than you were before, or you can let the situation overwhelm you and sink into depression. You are not defined by your circumstances but by your decisions. The good news is that conscious decisions make up for 40 percent of the factors influencing your happiness – which means that you have greater control over your own happiness than you might think.

HAPPINESS VS. SUCCESS

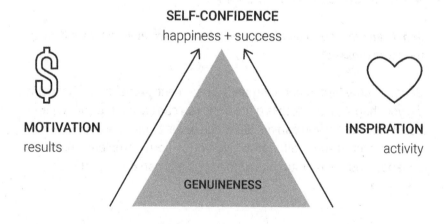

SELF-CONFIDENCE
happiness + success

MOTIVATION
results

INSPIRATION
activity

GENUINENESS

People often believe that success equals happiness. However, striving to achieve success or gain wealth (motivation) without also following your heart (inspiration) means chasing after something that will forever elude you. Motivation vs. inspiration is a recurring theme that we have already explored in previous chapters. Happiness leads to success, not the other way round. Successful people are often unhappy. A person who feels happy is likely to do well in all areas of their life. Research has actually proved that positively minded individuals tend to have a higher income than those who are not content in their life.[24]

Jan: *Working for Bill Gates and traveling with him was like having my own private research lab where I could study the correlation between success and happiness. Bill loved designing software; it was an endless source of inspiration for him and the meaning of his life. As the richest man in the world, he was happy – but when he started his own foundation and began donating to various charity projects (HIV research and treatment, Alzheimer's disease, humanitarian aid in Africa, education, etc.), he was even happier.*

Working with Bill, I realized that happiness was not a single, clearly defined point in time but rather a journey. Bill chose software design as his path in life, with the aim of making information technology accessible to everyone. When I joined Microsoft, Bill's vision of "a computer on every desk and in every home" was far from becoming reality. Today, people own multiple electronic devices, including tablets and smartphones.

Humans are social creatures who feel happy and fulfilled if they can make someone else happy. Bill Gates and his ex-wife Melinda have managed to achieve this through their charitable foundation.

Happiness is the pleasurable emotion you feel when you manage to fulfill your potential. However, no one is an island. A person's sense of happiness greatly depends on their ability to make other people happy.

MONEY VS. HAPPINESS

Money is a reward received for a certain activity. If you only focus on making money, regardless of whether you actually enjoy and/or believe in the work you perform, it will most likely not bring you the happiness you desire. Happiness is brought by performing the activity itself, which inspires you rather than motivating you to make even more money. If you have a talent for what you do for a living and enjoy what you do, money is a mere by-product of that. Unfortunately, it doesn't usually work the other way round. If all you enjoy in life is having a lot of money and the work you do is merely the means to an end, you will never be truly happy.

The so-called **Maslow's hierarchy of needs** is a classification system illustrating people's behavioral motivation. It is usually depicted in the form of a pyramid, with the most fundamental needs at the bottom.

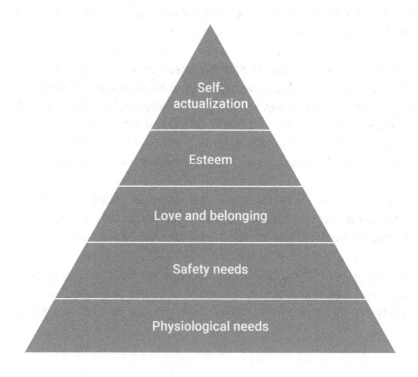

The bottom tiers of Maslow's pyramid include things that can be acquired for money: food, shelter, and so on. The second level of human needs involves the sense of safety. The third level is the human need to belong. The fourth level involves the need to feel respected, which also includes the need for self-esteem. The topmost level of the pyramid is the need for self-actualization.

If you focus on the lower tiers of Maslow's pyramid, there is a limit to what money can buy. Once a person covers their most fundamental needs, they feel the urge to fulfill the needs from the upper levels of the pyramid to achieve happiness. The lower levels are based on motivation, the upper levels, on inspiration.[25]

Self-actualization means performing activities we find fulfilling and that are able to induce flow state and genuine happiness. As long as the basic needs from the lower levels are covered, the material aspect becomes only secondary on this level.

Jan: *In the corporate world, employees often complain that their work does not bring them a sense of self-fulfillment or that their superiors are not interested in what they do. Such complaints usually result in getting a raise – but that's actually not what the employees asked for. They need the self-fulfillment their work can bring them in order to reach the top of Maslow's pyramid.*

American-Israeli teacher and writer Tal Ben-Shahar wrote the best-selling book *Happier* (yes, "Happier," not "Happiness"). In it, he claims that if we do what we like and enjoy, we can be a little happier every day. Happiness is a process, not a single point in time. It's important to realize that.

You may wonder why we are spending so much time discussing the connection between money and happiness in a book about developing children's potential. The answer is simple. Parents often pressure their children to maintain good grades or choose a "promising" major in college in order to acquire a lucrative profession, in the belief it will bring them happiness. They couldn't be more wrong.

Grades and results are often the only thing parents care about. Children are easily able to sense this, which compels them to start focusing on getting quick results in order to please their parents. This, however, puts them in a vicious circle which leads to a permanent rat race and burn-out, rather than true happiness. They might end up doing a high-paying job they actually hate.

Consider a child who loves animals and biology and keeps telling their parents that they would like to become a veterinarian. The parents, how-ever, keep pressuring them to go to law school, in the belief that being a lawyer is a much more prestigious and lucrative job. Depending on how assertive the child is, they may either become a happy veterinarian or an unhappy lawyer. Another child might actually want to become a lawyer, but their parents – both doctors – want them to follow in their footsteps. Every parent wants what they think is best for their child, and making good money provides a certain kind of freedom. Many young people, however, would gladly trade a high-paying job for the opportu-nity to travel the world. They value experience over financial security, and traveling represents a different kind of freedom.

Suggestion: Don't forget that today's young people can actually make good money through sharing their experiences on social media. Food bloggers, travel bloggers, photographers, and You-Tubers can acquire tremendous influence, simply through sha-ring their everyday lives. Their enthusiasm and passion can often inspire others to fulfill their own dreams.

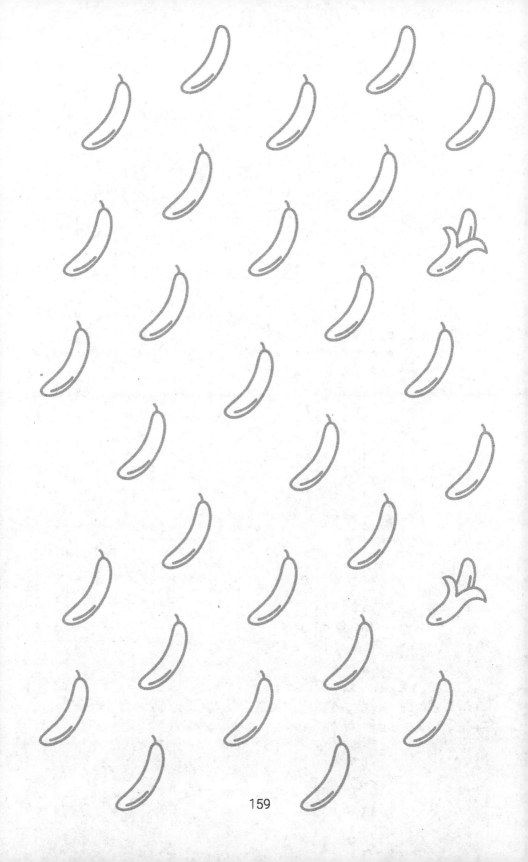

7

SELF-
EXPRESSION

FEAR TO SHOW OUR STRENGTHS

Looking at the general population of the Czech Republic, we can see a distinct dichotomy. The Czech people are usually capable of far more than they show. After all we have discussed so far, you may be able to guess the reason.

Many factors are at play: the Czech education system and a tendency toward strict parenting methods, as well as historical conditions. As a small country, the Czech Republic has almost always been controlled by its stronger neighbors. The Czech folklore, songs, and proverbs often reflect the Czechs' typical way of thinking. "He who does nothing spoils nothing." "Better a bird in the hand than two in the bush." "Better safe than sorry." "Great things come to those who wait." "Worth will show itself; no need to flaunt it."

A globalized world also means global competition on the job market. Today's Czech children will one day have to compete with people from all over the world. Nothing can prevent that – but we can help our children by raising them to be able to sell what they can do. Czech parents are quite skilled at developing their child's talents but not so good at teaching them how to assert themselves and show their strong points. The reticent, hesitant approach toward life and the emphasis on modesty and self-effacement has been bred into Czech people for generations, and it will not be easy to break out of the mold.

The Czech folktale of Johnny the Simpleton is an apt illustration of a typical Czech attitude. The protagonist is an ignorant sluggard, who is thrown out by his own parents for his indolence. Only then does he set out to find himself a bride – but not an ordinary bride, mind you: none other than a princess will do! By a clever stroke of luck, he manages to slay a dragon and get the princess – without actually doing anything much to accomplish it. The tale perpetuates a dangerous myth: it tells us that it's possible to get what we want without doing anything. Accomplishing your goals takes hard work and mental resilience. You won't win the Olympics by lazing about in bed all day.

WHY CZECHS CANNOT SELL THEIR CRAFT

Let's illustrate this problem with a simple chart.

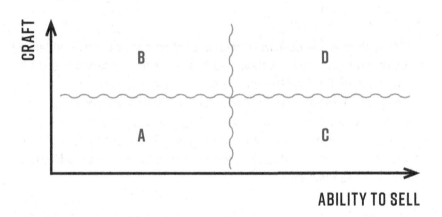

A craft is anything you are good at: playing ice hockey, singing, playing the piano, organizational skills... The ability to sell your craft depends on many factors but primarily on your communication skills.

The bottom-left quadrant includes people who are not really good at anything and cannot sell even the little that they **can** do. The top-left quadrant comprises those who possess a certain craft but cannot sell it. This is pretty much true for the majority of Czech people. They either restrict their craft to a private hobby or try to sell it but keep failing. The bottom-right quadrant includes those who are not particularly good at anything but who have the ability to sell even the little they can do. This includes people from a lot of countries. The top-right quadrant is the best one – people who have mastered a craft **and** the art to sell it.

People from Scandinavian countries often fall into this category – they are very good at what they do and even better at selling it. Czechs should do their best not to fall to the bottom-left quadrant but move to the top-right one.

Czech children are smart and talented and often grow up into world-class athletes or scientists. There could, however, be a lot more of them if parents were better able to work on improving both their self-confidence and self-assertion. It would be immensely beneficial if Czech schools started teaching students the art of elocution, which is currently not a standard part of the traditional school system. Children who are able to complete a complex team project will do anything to avoid presenting it to the audience. The unlucky one who has drawn the short straw then looks around helplessly and mutters something under their breath. Very few Czech children have the self-confidence to present the results of their work to their schoolmates. However, children from the US or from Scandinavian countries are usually more confident in presentation. They can present the results of their work because they learn to do so at school.

Adults are not much better. Thirty years after the Velvet Revolution, people still use the repressive methods of the communist era as an excuse, but generations born after the communist regime was overthrown are as bad at presenting their own work as their predecessors. People capable of selling their skills are few and far between, and the rare gifted speakers enjoy an almost celebrity-like status. The truth is that anyone, even the most introverted people, can learn to speak in front of an audience.

Parents often make the mistake of underestimating their introverted child. They are often happy the child has managed to say *something*, believing that they have reached their limits. However, the belief that only extroverted people can be truly charismatic speakers is equally mistaken. The only difference between an introverted and extroverted person is the source of their energy. Extroverted people draw energy from others; introverts draw it from within themselves. It may take an introverted person a bit longer to learn to speak in public, but they *can* do it; it just takes more effort. On the other hand, introverts may be far better than extroverts at written communication.

Jan: *I am an extroverted person, and it takes much more effort for me to write something than to say it.*

Both personality types can learn to speak in public equally well. What they both need are formal lessons in elocution: a subject that teaches both adults and children to speak, communicate, and debate. Today's children and young people are generally very poor debaters, unable to present clear arguments.

Jan: *My daughter Kristina only learned to debate once she started going to formal debating contests. These days, it's extremely hard to win a debate with her. She's very well read and knows how to choose the best arguments to support her position.*

To ensure a child's happiness, parents should encourage them to improve their talents but also to learn to present their skills to total strangers and assert themselves. There is nothing wrong with a child being able to describe what they like doing and what they are good at.

Cyril Höschl: My son Cyril has always been very money-oriented. He started making money designing software when he was 12 years old. I actually used to borrow money from him sometimes. He was not old enough to have his own bank account, so he had to use his older sister as a front. One day he came to me complaining that I gave his brother Patrik CZK 3.60 for a school notebook. "Aren't you ashamed?" I told him. "You're earning your own money. Why would you envy your brother a few korunas for a notebook?" His answer was very typical of him. "So, just to make it clear," he said, "Is being able to make my own money actually a bad thing? You want to punish me for it by not giving me money anymore? You're going to pay for my brother's school stuff but not for mine? Is making money a crime? Should I start buying my own food from now on? I just want you to explain it to me." I had no choice but to back off and give him the money.

"Selling a skill" doesn't always have to be taken literally. You can sell a skill by helping someone while using that particular skill. It means that you have shown others your talent and ability and improved their life while doing it.

HELPING CHILDREN LEARN TO EXPRESS THEMSELVES

Schools don't do enough to teach children to present their skills and talents. That's why parents should try to practice and discuss this ability at home with their children.

Many parents simply give their child instructions/offer a lot of information and advice on how to do this based on their own experience, but they don't give their child a chance to work it out on their own initiative. This approach is known as mentoring. The child will be able to follow the instructions repeatedly but will not internalize them. Once they find themselves in a situation where the parental instructions do not apply, they will not know what to do. They may become withdrawn or shy.

Once you stop giving your child advice and instructions and start asking them questions, they will learn to find answers on their own. Trying to find a solution on their own engages their brain much more than simply accepting an adult's advice. This approach is known as coaching. A coach helps the person being coached find their own way of doing things and approaches them as a partner rather than as a superior. (More on coaching and mentoring in Chapter 8.)

Children need to learn the art of debate, but the school and/or home environment do not provide enough space for them to share their thoughts. Engaging in a discussion helps the child improve their reasoning and listening skills and teaches them to describe their feelings and thoughts and defend their wants and needs. Children growing up in an authoritative environment are not given the opportunity to learn these skills. If you ask such a child, for example, to explain how they solved a certain problem, they simply can't do it.

Kateřina: *This is a problem we come across quite often at our workshops. We give children a simple visual problem to solve, such as images that are somehow related, in order to improve their associative thinking. Even children who are able to find the right answer find it difficult to explain their reasoning. Some will attempt it but are not able to communicate it in a way that others would understand.*

Schools put a great emphasis on results, not the process needed to achieve them. They don't encourage children to describe the thought process they used to get the results and think about the approach they chose (visual, analytical, or logical). At our workshops, we try to guide children through the entire solution process and trace back their own reasoning. How did they approach the problem? What did they think about first and what next? We go through the entire process and ask the children what they found interesting or challenging along the way. In the end, we ask the children to describe their thought process to other participants. Many children find this difficult because they are not used to doing things that way. They don't know how to *think about thinking*, which means they are unable to share their thought processes with anyone else. To master this ability, they need to practice thinking about their thought process and practice their communication skills and elocution.

A child who is happy to have mastered a certain skill or solved a problem will gladly go through the entire process with their teacher or parent. This both teaches them to present their talent and helps them consolidate the skill in their brain, gradually turning it into a strength (as in the example about a child bringing home a picture they drew in school when we discussed feedback in Chapter 5).

A great, world-changing idea is worth nothing if you are not able to explain and present it in a simple enough manner for everyone to understand. Your project will never come to fruition if you are not able to get investors on your side.

Most investors' thinking is pretty simple: if they decide to invest a dollar, they want to see it turn into five – or even ten – dollars within the next few years. They don't care if your idea is going to change the world as we know it; all they want is a return on their investment. Potential entrepreneurs presenting their projects are often unable to grasp this basic fact and present their ideas in a concise, persuasive manner.

To present a project, or actually deliver any prearranged spoken presentation, you need a carefully prepared draft. In school, children learn to make outlines for their written compositions but hardly ever do they learn to organize their speech. Such an outline is also known as a "strawman draft." It's a carefully structured script outlining the key aspects of a speech or proposal. Today's children may learn to create PowerPoint documents to accompany their spoken presentations, but that will not teach them to master the art of elocution and articulate expression.

EXERCISE: STRAW-MAN DRAFT

Before each presentation, your child (with your help) should create a simple, structured draft to help them deliver the presentation clearly and concisely. When they have mastered the skill sufficiently, they can start making such drafts on their own.

1. Define your goal

Encourage the child to define what the goal of their presentation is. Do they want to entertain their audience, make others embrace their vision, educate, or inform?

2. Analyze your audience

Your child should find out what kind of audience they are going to speak to. Children or adults? Friends or strangers? Knowing their audience can help the child plan both the topic of their presentation and the way they are going to deliver it (formal or informal). There is no need to push your child to speak properly and formally. The important thing is to be relaxed and deliver their message in a clear, comprehensible manner. They can work on improving their speech and language gradually.

3. Plan your presentation

It's useful to put down the key points your child wants to talk about. There is no need to write out the full speech, just the gist of what they want to say.

We also recommend that the child learns and practices the introduction and conclusion to their presentation beforehand. This will give them the necessary self-confidence and allow them to relax. The conclusion should summarize the entire presentation. It's also good to include a joke or a few witty remarks to end the presentation in a confident, engaging manner. However, the child should not write down and memorize the entire presentation – if they happen to for-get something, their Monkey could start pan-icking and disrupt the whole presentation.

Planning the presentation:

A. Choose your topic

Encourage your child to choose something they like or enjoy doing. If they have been assigned a topic, help the child find an aspect or part of the topic they already know, or con-nect it to something they feel emotionally con-nected to – through a story or an experience, for example.

B. Make a list of key points

Put together a list of all ideas the child has on the subject. Write down anything the child can think of that they find important, interesting, or entertaining for their intended audience.

C. Organize your key points

Now you need to sort the child's ideas and thoughts and connect them logically with the information the child should impart to others ("wrap the facts in a story").

D. Conclusion

The conclusion should summarize the entire presentation, highlight the salient facts, point the listeners toward additional sources, or lighten the atmosphere with a joke or witty remark (depending on the topic).

HOW WE LEARN

People learn their whole life. Even once you get a job, you still need to keep learning new things, and learning becomes harder the older you are – and even more difficult if you are not sufficiently self-aware to know your learning style and what makes learning easy for you.

Teachers in school give children information with the simple instruction to learn, memorize, and remember it. If you manage to find out, however, how your brain best retains information (using visual or logical thinking, linking the new information to other knowledge to fixate it, etc.), you will save yourself a lot of effort, and learning will be easier for you even in older age.

Jan: *I am a visual learner – I remember things better if I see them written down or printed. However, making handwritten notes helps me to retain information even better. Some people only need to look at a printed text once and they can recite it word for word.*

Everyone learns a little differently, using different techniques and perceptions, depending on what type of learner they are and what they find easiest. Children should try exploring various ways of learning things, as well as their own thinking. Self-awareness is an essential part of the learning process. Most schools, however, do not teach children how to learn. Many people believe that the most important part of the learning process is the information we are able to memorize, but, in fact, it is far more important to use that information to discern our own learning process. In today's world, we can retrieve pretty much any information we need within seconds; even little children are now able to use Google and Wikipedia with ease. The crucial thing, however, is to learn to work with the information we find: verify it for relevance and veracity, track its sources, and connect it in a logical manner.

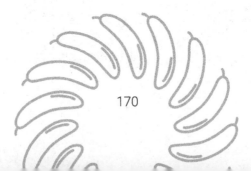

LEARNING AND FEAR OF FAILURE

When a child is under stress (before a written test or an oral exam, for example), their Monkey starts acting up and disrupts their ability to concentrate. Even if the child has studied a lot and knows the material, they naturally get nervous and start making up various disaster scenarios. Adults experience the same thing before an important event or task (like a project presentation). In moments like this, the brain starts producing cortisol, a hormone which hinders our verbal abilities, among other things. People whose brain is flooded by cortisol can start stammering or even rambling incoherently. Cortisol also blocks the ability to recall learned information from the subconscious. Under stress, you are thinking in a sort of haze. You can hardly stutter out a sentence, wondering where everything you have remembered so well just a moment ago has gone.

Overcome by nerves, some children have trouble reading text written in horizontal lines. This might be connected with the fact that reading (and writing) in lines is closely linked to spoken language. You could try to help your child by writing the words or math problem in a vertical column instead of a horizontal line.

Suggestion: If your child is prone to panicking or fits of nervousness when solving math problems, try writing the problem in a vertical column instead of a horizontal line. This does not put as much strain on the brain's center of logic and makes it easier for the child to work out the solution. Still, it's far more important for the child to form a habit which will prevent the Monkey from acting up in stressful situations. (More on this in the section How to Control Your Monkey later in this chapter.)

If a child needs to master a skill they are not particularly good at, it's a good idea to alternate it with something they can do easily and enjoy to keep them inspired. This obviously doesn't apply to a single math problem but to a long-term project/activity the child needs to learn or accomplish. You can't let the child work on such a task continuously. Constant focus on something they are not good at puts the child under prolonged stress, which causes regular, excessive production of stress hormones cortisol and adrenaline, whereas the production of happiness hormones, serotonin and dopamine, drops considerably. This induces anxiety and may lead to the onset of depression. If you don't let the child do anything they enjoy or have a talent for, they can never get into flow state, and stress hormones will eventually overflow their brain.

Supervising the child or waiting impatiently for them to finish the task will not help. Instead, you should encourage the child to take a break and do something else entirely. After a short break, they will be able to get back in the present moment much more easily.

Suggestion: Don't force your child to slave over something they are not good at. Alternate working on the child's weaknesses with things they are good at and enjoy doing.

No one can stay in flow state 100 percent of the time. Occasional stress is quite normal – it's prolonged stress that causes problems. Long-term stress reduces the brain's production of serotonin and dopamine. Stiffening of the neck muscles is also a frequent symptom. The mind and body are closely connected, and emotions can have a physical impact on a person's health. Positive emotions make you feel physically better; negative emotions, such as fear or stress, can have a harmful effect on your health. It's important to be aware of your emotions and be able to handle them. Parents often have a hard time admitting that their child's health issues could have been triggered mentally.

Mental discomfort can eventually manifest as a physical symptom. The same thing can happen if you are forced to do something you are not good at for an extended period.

FLOW AND OPTIMAL PERFORMANCE

Experts have long believed that to deliver the best possible performance, the human brain needs to operate at very high brainwave frequencies. Research has proved the opposite: the brain performs best at low (alpha or theta) frequencies.

The vertical axis denotes strain, i.e., the difficulty a task or activity presents for a person. The horizontal axis shows talent, i.e., the skills and aptitudes a person possesses to perform the task/activity.

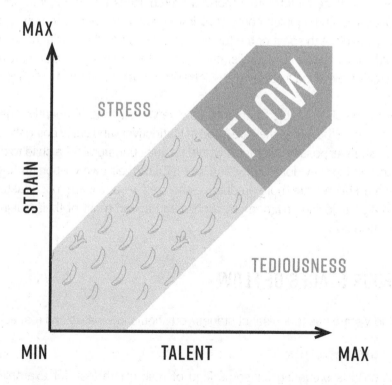

When does flow occur? Flow state occurs when you are performing a task/activity that is very demanding but that you have a great aptitude for, so rather than hard work, it represents a challenge. Flow state cannot be induced if you are doing something you struggle with and find stressful or something that is too easy for your advanced skills.

Research indicates that once an individual reaches flow state, two important changes occur in the brain's frontal cortex:

Changed time perception: when you do something you enjoy, you lose sense of time.

The amygdala is disabled: your Monkey, which tends to act up and offer disaster scenarios in order to protect you against danger or failure, stays dormant.

Both of these factors are important prerequisites for getting into flow. Once you find yourself completely immersed in the here and now, you don't think of the past or the future, fully focused on the task at hand. In order to achieve this mental state, however, the brain needs to operate at a fairly slow alpha frequency (8–12 Hz) or an even slower theta (4–8 Hz).

A happy child is able to get into flow very easily and frequently. They recognize the things they are good at instinctively and enjoy doing them as often as possible. In fact, it would be quite unnatural for a child to do something they don't like or find stressful of their own volition. In flow state, children are more productive and creative and learn much faster. In a safe, loving environment, a child can spend most of their waking time in flow.

FOUR STAGES OF FLOW

Flow state has four distinct stages you should internalize and respect.

I. PREPARATION

A child is preparing for some kind of task (math test, for example). Their brain is in full gear, operating at a high frequency.

2. RELAXATION

This stage occurs right before the task starts. It helps to relax, stop thinking about the task at hand, and focus on the here and now.

3. FLOW

Time of the actual performance – doing an activity a child is good at. The brain produces four "happiness hormones" – endorphin, dopamine, serotonin, and oxytocin (remember the so-called "happiness chemicals" from Chapter 6?). Flow can be loosely defined as the "combination of luck and success."

4. RESTORATION

The child's brain is now at rest, purifying itself of the chemicals it has produced in flow state. Flow is an addictive condition: the more time you spend in it, the more you want to keep spending there. The restorative stage could be described as a sort of withdrawal stage, but it's extremely important. A period of recuperation between each flow state is necessary for the brain to purge itself of the chemicals it has produced (ideally during sleep). Both your mind and body need to rest after an exhausting performance. If you do not allow yourself to recuperate, you may eventually slide into depression.

~~~~~~

The Czech high school graduation exam has written and oral parts. For the day of the written examination, a student is primed and ready and spends the entire assignment in flow state. If, however, they do not get enough sleep before the oral part of the exam, they can no longer achieve flow state – their brain has not yet purged itself of the chemicals produced during the previous flow. The student's heart rate increases and their Monkey is active, causing them to be less focused and speak faster. The result will most likely not be as good as if the student could get into flow.

~~~~~~

Let's look at this **simplified model of the brain** and discover how the brain's performance is tied to flow state and optimal performance.

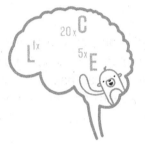

L = LOGIC

C = COMPUTER

E = EMOTIONS

The neocortex is the part of the brain responsible for **logical thinking**. The "speed" at which the neocortex operates is very low; we will assign it the value of 1. The section of the brain responsible for **emotional responses** includes the amygdala ("the Monkey") and operates at the relative speed of 5. Any information the brain receives has to be processed by the amygdala first. The Monkey evaluates every stimulus for potential danger. If it deems the particular stimulus as safe, it lets the brain absorb it without any hitch. If it decides the stimulus could present a threat, it makes you nervous and initiates the atavistic "fight-or-flight" response. The part of the brain we have called a computer is the **subconscious**, which is much faster than the logical and emotional part of the brain (we have assigned this the relative speed of 20). When assessing any new situation for potential danger, the Monkey consults the subconscious. A well-stored subconscious therefore has the potential to calm the Monkey before it can start acting up. Like a computer, the subconscious does not distinguish between true and untrue information – feeding it the right kind of information is therefore extremely important.[26]

A child is working on a math test, completely immersed in flow state. Once they realize they only have ten minutes to go, their Monkey starts panicking. The brain's logical center is too slow and won't be much help. This is where the subconscious can step in: as long as the child has practiced solving the problems enough, their subconscious is stored with sufficient data to inform the Monkey that it is perfectly possible to solve two more problems in those ten remaining minutes. Without a sufficient drill to back them up, the child gets nervous; their brain starts releasing cortisol and adrenaline and prevents them from focusing. The Monkey has managed to hijack their flow state.

UTILIZING YOUR TALENTS – GETTING INTO FLOW

Every child is born with a certain genetically inherited set of talents. Those talents represent potential; it is up to the child to unlock it. The more time and effort the child invests in their talent, the more they practice and read about people with similar gifts, the more likely it is that the talent will turn into a strength (see the formula $T \times I = S$ in Chapter 4). If a child takes their time working on an activity, excels at it, and enjoys doing it, they are sending quality data to their subconscious. Whenever the child finds himself in a stressful situation, this "winner" data will be able to calm his Monkey. Spending too much effort improving weaknesses sends "loser" data to the subconscious and feeds the Monkey. Working on weaknesses prevents the child from reaching flow state. In the long-term perspective, spending too much time on weaknesses might prevent the child from outright failure but will never turn them into a champion.

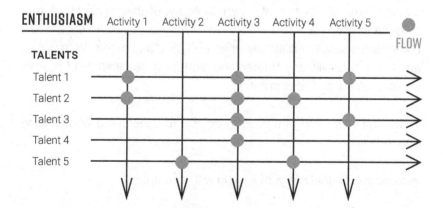

When parents force their child to perform tasks they are not talented at and do not enjoy, all the negative information and emotion related to such activities go directly to the child's subconscious. The child forms a negative emotional connection toward such activities, and his brain forms synapses reinforcing that connection. Unfortunately, many parents do this, crushing their child's talents before they can fully develop.

KNOWING YOUR OWN MIND

Did you know you could manage your own thoughts, controlling what to send down to your subconscious and what to keep out?

The technique, known as positive psychology, is quite easy to learn. Unfortunately, most people are not even aware of it. Ninety percent of parents attending our workshops are not used to thinking this way. Those who have never seen a therapist can find out about it from books, on the internet, or at a workshop or lecture.

Jan: *I've had ample personal experience with positive psychology. I've learned from experts and studied the method quite extensively.*

Negative thoughts and emotions make you feel bad. Sometimes mood swings cause you to feel fine one moment and down the next. This is especially true for women in the course of their menstrual cycle – a single "wrong" reaction at a certain phase of their cycle can turn a mild-mannered lady into a shrew. What should you do in such situations? Some people will simply write it off as a "bad mood." With this as an excuse, they will stay irritated and grumpy all day, instead of searching for the cause of their irritation.

To control your mind, you need to be able to understand what's going on inside it.

How do you do that? First of all, you will need time.

We may think hard, but we hardly ever think about **the way** we think. If you don't explore your own thought process, you can't make any positive changes to your attitude.

We all have our low moments. It's important to acknowledge your feelings and realize that your current state of mind is not ideal. Only when you realize how you're actually feeling can you start working on improving your bad mood. Some people try to suppress their negative feelings. Others won't even think of stopping to ponder their emotional state. *How am I feeling today? Why am I acting this way? What's the reason? Do I really want to behave like that?* Those are the questions people should be asking themselves.

Some people may be easily offended but feel too proud to try and resolve the situation. You might get mad at your neighbor for the clutter in his yard, but instead of talking to him about it, your anger keeps festering until you start an argument with your neighbor the first chance you get.

Jan: I used to get angry easily, and my Monkey would always look for more reasons to get even angrier. Nowadays I am able to stop this onslaught of negative thoughts and look back to see where they came from.

Suggestion: Whenever things don't turn out the way you want or when you're beset by a bad mood, take a mental step back. Ask yourself: *Do I really want to feel this way? What's happening to me? What can I do to find my inner equilibrium again?* If your irritation has been caused by someone else (partner, neighbor), you need to ask *them* those questions. Tell them what they did and how it makes you feel so you can restore your mental balance. If you allow your emotions to take control of your actions, it will make it harder to step back and look at the situation dispassionately. Few people realize that their state of mind is something they can actually control.

Learn to control your Monkey by focusing on your breathing pattern and returning to the present moment. Instead of nursing your grievances and thinking about payback, you will be able to keep your cool even in the most emotionally charged situations.

As parents, you have no doubt experienced countless situations with your child that have tested your patience and self-control. The child misbehaves and you lose your temper and start shouting (or do something else that you may later regret). Through your parenting methods, you can have a certain degree of influence over your child's behavior, but that does not give you a sure fire guarantee that the child will react to every situation the way you want them to. The only thing you *can* influence is your own behavior toward your child in an unexpected situation. Parents are often influenced by their own childhood experience. If you fail to realize that you are free to choose how to respond to your child's unacceptable behavior, you will probably react in a similar way to your own parents. Only when you manage to realize that your reaction was excessive or unwanted can you start breaking those behavioral patterns. Remember that children follow their parents' example. If you are prone to anger and irritation, your children may soon begin to react in a similar manner.

HOW TO CONTROL YOUR MONKEY

To make sure your child delivers the best possible performance, they need to learn to pacify and control their Monkey. There are various techniques and exercises which can help your child do that.

Whenever the Monkey starts jumping frantically from thought to thought, the first thing you need to do is **get back to the here and now**. As we discussed earlier, when you are immersed in the present moment the Monkey is dormant, which allows you to get in flow state while performing a task or an activity. Once you start thinking about the past or making premature conclusions about the future, your Monkey wakes up and starts affecting your performance. The Monkey is governed by fear – which is what it has been designed for. A conscious return to the here and now can calm it down.

Cyril Höschl: My daughter Kristina is a paramedic, working either in an ambulance van or a medical helicopter. She often finds herself in dramatic situations: she's saved skiers in the Alps, been to Afghanistan with Doctors Without Borders, climbed Mount Everest, and parachuted from an airplane. Situations like this require quick thinking and snap decisions; there's no time for sentiment or long-winded contemplation. You have to make the right decision without thinking about it, which requires a great deal of mental resilience. She often works in terrible conditions, performing difficult medical interventions outside – on the road, in storms and mud, surrounded by curious bystanders. I once asked her if she felt stressed out. She told me she had two options. She could either do nothing and the person would die, or she could do something and the patient may still die but might not. She's giving them a chance. A bad thing has already happened to them, so whatever she does will only improve their situation.

~~~~~~~~~~~~~~~~~~~~~~~~

Sometimes all you need is a simple reminder:

I am here and now.

Other times your Monkey will require a more ingenious method to calm down.

In the following section you will find several tried-and-tested ways of calming down the Monkey that both you and your children may find useful. Most of the exercises can be performed anytime and anywhere. Next time your child is taking a test and has only ten minutes left to go, some of these methods may help them stay relaxed.

BREATHING EXERCISES

Breathing is a tool that is always available to return you to the present moment. It never looks back into the past or to the future. It's always in the here and now.

EXERCISE: BOX BREATHING METHOD (FEED YOUR MONKEY)

When a child is nervous, their brain produces cortisol and adrenaline, and the Monkey is frantic. The child's breath is shallow, and they may start trembling inwardly. Teach the child to remember that breathing properly can help.

A very useful exercise is the so-called breathing method, developed by the American Navy SEALs. Here's how it's done:

Breathe in through your nose while slowly counting to five (your child may try doing it for just three seconds). Hold your breath and slowly count to five (three) again. Then slowly breathe out through your nose, counting to five (three). Hold your breath again for five (three) seconds. Repeat the exercise at least five times.

Slow, deep breaths trick the Monkey into thinking the (imaginary) threat has passed. To make it easier for your child to imagine, explain to them that breathing is a way to feed the Monkey so it will calm down. Only a well-fed Monkey (that has been given a banana, for example) can go back to sleep. Once the child is relaxed enough, they can go back to whatever they've been doing before.

You can help the child do the exercise by reciting a sentence. "I'm giving [breathe in] my Monkey [hold your breath] a banana [breathe out]." Children will remember the exercise more easily and find it more fun.

When a child is about to switch from one activity to another, it's a good idea to practice deep breathing for about 30 seconds. Those 30 seconds are like 30 present moments that give the child a much-needed pause to relax.

BODY SCAN

In this exercise, you go over your entire body in your mind and make yourself aware of each of its parts.

SELF-EXPRESSION

EXERCISE: BODY SCAN

If you're standing, sit down; if you're sitting, stand up. Simply choose a different position to the one you were in when your Monkey started acting up. Feel your big toes. Move them a little and relax them consciously.

If you're wearing shoes, use your fingers. Stretch your arms forward and wiggle your fingers. Check that you still have all of them.

For some people, this is already sufficient to make them relax enough to be able to go back to their previous activity.

If you are extremely agitated and need more time to calm down, try "scanning" your entire body from your toes to the top of your head. Make sure everything is in its place and fully in the here and now.

This is a great calming-down exercise. Your body, just like your breath, is always in the present moment. The only body that is in the past is a dead one, and there is no body yet in the future. Everything inside your body is happening in the here and now.

ACT OF THANKFULNESS

For an untrained brain, it's quite common to keep mulling over the one thing you've failed at during the day and ignore the five you did right. You may have difficulty falling asleep or keep tossing and turning all night. The reason this happens is because you can't accept yourself for who you really are. You keep raking over your past mistakes and thinking about things you can't change. You may even be feeling sorry for yourself. The point is that, in such moments, you are not fully in the present. In the here and now, you have no trouble accepting yourself just as you are. (Obviously, that doesn't mean you should stop wanting to improve.)

EXERCISE: ACT OF THANKFULNESS

Before you fall asleep, think of three things you did right or that made you happy that day and give thanks for them. In the morning, right after you wake up, think of three things you are looking forward to that day and give thanks for them as well. Take this short moment of gratitude to give thanks for things that you might be taking for granted and encourage your children to do the same.

You can even turn this into a nightly ritual with your children: every day before bed, each of you shares three things you are thankful for. Some children are eager to tell their parents what they enjoyed most during the day and are curious to know what their parents liked. It need not be a fancy adventure – you can be thankful even for the most trivial but pleasing things.

This exercise can help you reset the brain to stop focusing on failures and start seeing the world from a more positive perspective.

Jan: *When I started speaking in public, more than 20 years ago, I would always scan the audience for that one person who was not paying attention. My Monkey would immediately go frantic and make me start speculating: "No one is listening to me. Perhaps what I'm saying is not all that interesting. Or maybe it's my poor English." My brain was flooded with cortisol and adrenaline; I grew nervous and felt even worse. After a while I realized what I was doing and consciously tried to change it.*

Today, if I see someone in the audience who's not paying attention, I simply look elsewhere. I am aware of the way my Monkey reacts and I know how to control it. You need to be aware of the problem to be able to handle it.

Carrie Kirsten is a successful Czech YouTuber. For the hundreds of thousands of likes under each of her videos, she would get perhaps ten hateful comments – but those ten hates were what she focused on. I explained to her that she should focus on the people who like her and pay attention to the positive reactions rather than the negative ones. Ninety percent of internet haters have fake profiles. Why should you give any weight to the words of someone who's too chicken to write under their real name or give any kind of constructive criticism?

MINDFULNESS

Mindfulness is an extremely useful technique which allows you to fully experience the present moment, without overanalyzing your thoughts, dwelling on past mistakes, or worrying about the future.

Staying firmly anchored in the present moment is something even adults often struggle with. You keep thinking about a hundred different things, feeling that it would be a waste of time to focus on a simple activity you can do on autopilot (driving a car, cutting up vegetables...).

Various theories try to convince us that our brain has been designed to handle multiple tasks at once. That is actually untrue. You might think you can handle several things at once, but in fact you are just jumping from one thing to another, losing your focus over and over again. Doing two things simultaneously exhausts your brain so much it's as if you haven't slept for 36 hours straight. A surgeon operating on a patient cannot do two things at once. If they did, it might cost the patient their life. Multitasking is simply impossible in some professions. Still, many people will do two or more things at once, even though they are well aware of how dangerous it is. Some people make calls or even text while driving, which is the worst thing you can do.

Suggestion: Forget about multitasking. Save your mental energy and always focus on the task at hand. Stay fully immersed in the present moment and take notice of everything you're doing or that's going on around you, without evaluating it in any way. Obviously, you can't stay in the here and now all day, but find a few minutes every day to practice your mindfulness techniques. You can do it while eating, brushing your teeth, doing dishes, driving your car, or going for a walk.

EXERCISE: BODY AWARENESS

Take notice of your child performing a simple activity – painting a picture, putting together a jigsaw puzzle, watering the garden. When you notice your child is not as fully immersed in the task as they could be, try using a code word that you've both agreed upon ("Body inventory! NOW!," for example).

The purpose of this is to make the child stop and become aware of what they are doing and of their own feelings while doing it. Are they enjoying it, fully immersed in the here and now, or are their thoughts wandering?

Try this exercise both with your children and on your own. Mindfulness training is something both parents and children can benefit from.

Jan: *Ten years ago, I would always listen to music or something else when I went out for a jog. That wasn't mindfulness. I was always paying attention to things other than the here and now. Nowadays, I try to do nothing but run for half of the time and listen to things going on around me for the other half (birds singing, trees rustling...). Staying in the present moment helps improve my concentration.*

Kateřina: *My four-year-old border collie, Bubbles, is a great mindfulness coach. She teaches me to stop and relax amid the hustle and bustle of my workday. Sometimes I just plop down on the ground next to her and then we play and cuddle, or I simply talk to her. It helps me sort out my thoughts.*

Today's children have trouble simply staying still. They are easily distracted and have trouble focusing. They are unable to relax, pay attention to their own mind and body, and listen to the silence. Many adults have the same problem. Can you simply enjoy the silence? Try teaching your children to stay still and focus from preschool age.

EXERCISE: STAYING STILL

Children in Montessori preschools practice staying still by sitting down in a circle. The teacher will then drop a pin or a bead or some other tiny item. The children know that if they want to hear the pin or bead drop, they must be very quiet. If they keep chattering, they won't hear the "magic sound." "Did you all hear the pin drop?" the teacher will then ask. This makes the children realize that sometimes they need to stay very still, even if only for a few seconds.

You can try this exercise with one child or several children, on the floor or at a table. It can be you or the children dropping the item. Try to switch the items you use to produce different sounds. Children love pouring or sifting through things (such as beans, buttons, or beads). You can also try running a wet finger along the rim of a glass. Exercises like this one make the child realize the uniqueness of the present moment.

Suggestion: Encourage your child to try out various techniques to stay still and quiet enough to become aware of the silence. You can be as creative as you want, depending on what works best for your child.

You can, for example, ring a bell right before dinner every day. At the sound of the bell, both parents and children must stay absolutely still for a few moments. If you're also doing the thankfulness ritual with your children, you can include the moment of silence right before that. It will set the mood and allow you to contemplate the events of the day.

It's important to stay completely still for a moment and only then proceed to another activity.

Approximately 60,000 thoughts run through an average person's head every day. Research has proved that out of those 60,000 thoughts, 90 percent are completely repetitive. Some of them can be set off by the most trivial things. If you are aware of what triggered a specific thought, you can dismiss it easily. Unfortunately, many people are not able to trace back the trigger which has set off a train of negative thoughts and emotions. Once you let that first trivial stimulus set you off, it can trigger a bad mood for the rest of the day.

Try to train your brain to search for the original thought triggers. It will work wonders for your state of mind.

Controlling your mind will allow you to stay in the present moment. It's the only way you can achieve flow state. If you can't control your thoughts, your Monkey will not allow you to get into flow. This is not an act of willful sabotage – protecting you is what your Monkey was designed for.

If you dwell too much on the past or the future, you can't very well be mindful of the present. Whenever you are able to control your thoughts, your ego (and your Monkey) gets sidetracked, allowing you to take notice of everything around you. Once that happens, you will probably start noticing how fast things change. Being aware of the fleetingness of things will make you realize that there's no point in getting overly focused on results or material things. It's far better to focus on the present moment because only in the here and now can you change the outcome of your effort. You can only be genuine in the present. That's why children are so natural and unaffected – they mostly stay in the present. Adults often try to follow some arbitrary rules of what they should or should not be doing.

Cyril Höschl: Swiss developmental psychologist Jean Piaget postulated that thinking is internalized behavior. A small child first acts, then thinks. What happens to the vase on the table if I pull down the tablecloth? The child has to actually pull down the cloth to be able to imagine the outcome. The ability to imagine possible consequences only comes with experience. That's why you need to watch over small children constantly – they act before thinking. The cognitive process can therefore be described as internalized behavior. Actual motor acts start happening symbolically in the child's mind.

MEDITATION

Meditation is a conscious effort to get your brainwaves to operate on alpha frequency. Proper, regular meditation trains the brain to calm down the Monkey. The longer your brain operates on an alpha or theta frequency, the less active the amygdala (i.e., your Monkey) is. Some scientists even claim that regular meditation causes the amygdala to shrink.

There are various methods of meditation, but all of them have a common goal: to purge the mind of all thoughts. In breathing meditation, you focus on your breath pattern and ignore any distracting thoughts. Mantra meditation involves using a certain word or sentence that you constantly repeat, either aloud or inwardly, and you focus your mind exclusively on it. It's important that the mantra be just a set of sounds without any sense or meaning. Only then can the brain ignore it and stop producing thoughts based on the words.

Beginners will find that their mind is constantly buzzing with thoughts. It will be very hard to get rid of them completely. To start with, try not to dwell on the thoughts running through your mind; simply let them flow. After regular practice, you will be able to purge your mind of all thoughts in a matter of moments.

EXERCISE: BREATHING MEDITATION

Sit comfortably. Focus on breathing in and breathing out. If your mind gets flooded with distracting thoughts, do not dwell on them or analyze them. Always try to focus back on your breath.

EXERCISE: MANTRA MEDITATION

If you find it hard to simply follow your breath for a prolonged time, try adding the so-called So Hum Mantra. It will help you focus on your breath and prevent your thoughts from wandering.

As you inhale, silently repeat the word "So." As you exhale, silently repeat the word "Hum." Make your exhales longer than your inhales. Continue breathing slowly and regularly and repeat the mantra silently.

Mindfulness and meditation are useful mental techniques to keep your brainwaves on an alpha frequency and calm your Monkey.

There are monks who have spent more than 10,000 hours in meditation during their lives. It would be near impossible to make them lose their temper. Their amygdala is completely subdued – an electroencephalogram (EEG) would most likely show that it has completely atrophied.

Getting into a flow state and staying in it can become a learned habit. If you manage to get your Monkey under control, you can get into flow far more often – which will also make you far happier.

EXERCISE: FEAR INVENTORY

This exercise helps children realize the connection between their body and their emotions. If they become aware of how their body and mind are intertwined, they can stop their Monkey from acting up in stressful situations. The exercise should also help your child understand that once you are overcome by fear, you should remove the cause of the fear instead of wasting your energy on suppressing it.

Step 1: How to recognize you are afraid.

"When my teeth and fists are clenched, I am probably angry because of something that provoked me."

Everyone experiences fear a little differently. You can discuss the different feelings with your child.

Step 2: Fill out the "Fear Inventory" form with your child, listing various physical reactions to fear. Check those reactions your child remembers having (not everyone experiences all of those reactions). This may help your child become more aware of their reactions. Whenever they get afraid, you can go back to the form together and discuss their reactions.

FEAR INVENTORY

When I am afraid:

- my mouth goes dry

- my mouth is suddenly full of saliva

- my face is flushed

- spots appear on my face and neck

- I get goose bumps

- my hair stands on end

- my hands get clammy

- I break into a sweat all over

- my voice changes

- I get restless

- I can feel my stomach

- I tremble all over

Step 3: Talk to your child about recognizing fear and ways to get rid of it. Finally, you can discuss what you have gained from the exercise.

- What is the most important thing you have learned?

- Do you understand how fear affects your body?

- What do you want to do most when you are afraid?

- When would you rather run? When would you choose to attack instead?

- Which situations make you the most afraid?

- Are you afraid to speak in front of people?

RECHARGING

There are four levels of energy a person should try to maintain. To keep our energy levels up on all four levels, you need to cultivate specific energy-recharging habits.

FOUR ENERGY LEVELS

PHYSICAL ENERGY

Physical energy depends on the nutrients you provide to your body, i.e., what you eat and drink. A balanced, healthy diet is the key. Many foodstuffs and beverages are over-processed and contain an unhealthy amount of sugar. As parents, you should be mindful of what your children drink and eat and ensure that they have a healthy diet. The body needs sugar to function but not the kind of sugar you put in your coffee or baked desserts. What you need are simple carbohydrates (monosaccharides) like glucose and fructose, which naturally occur in fruit or honey or (in a much lower amount) polysaccharides found in cereals or potatoes. Too much sugar can actually be harmful for the body and sap it of energy. A child who eats chocolate cereals for breakfast and has a candy bar for a snack will have almost no energy to think properly during their school lessons. This is because high amounts of sugar trigger a rapid increase and a subsequent sharp decrease in blood sugar level. For optimal performance, the blood sugar level should stay balanced throughout the day.

Another big mistake that parents often make is letting their children drink sweet soda, tea, or syrup all day. There is nothing wrong with drinking a sweetened beverage once in a while, but most of a person's liquid intake should be water only. The human body is around 60 percent water and needs to replenish all the water it loses by breathing, speaking, or sweating. No sugar or flavors are needed.

Make sure that your children's diet is as healthy and balanced as possible.

Exercise is another important way to replenish physical energy.

Kateřina: *When I was little, I would come home, throw my bookbag in the corner, spend as little time doing homework as possible, and then go out. And by going out I mean running around the park or playground, playing games and sports, climbing trees, or simply making mischief. All of this meant we got plenty of exercise. Even getting all your friends to go out with you involved going to all the houses in the neighborhood, ringing the bell, and asking their parents to let them go out. Today, with all the social media and digital devices we have, children feel no need to actually go out – they can just meet in the online world. I'm not trying to say that parents should confiscate their children's phones and send them out to play under threat of punishment. Digital technology and social media are a part of our world now. There's no way to avoid them unless you want to live in the woods as a hermit. Instead, parents should nurture their children's love for sports and find ways for them to exercise and enjoy themselves at the same time.*

Today's children come home from school, throw their bookbag in the corner (so far, so good) – and then sit down and log on to their laptop, tablet, or cell phone and stay glued to it all afternoon. Physical exercise is extremely important, both for the body and the mind.

Not all families are the same, obviously: many children are involved in various after-school sports clubs or play a sport actively. There are children, however, who spend five or more hours a day glued to a monitor. This can have fatal consequences for both their mental and physical development. The Czech government, along with sports coaches, is currently trying to expand the weekly Phys Ed classes to three hours instead of two but, compared to the long hours the children spend motionless online, even three hours a week is not enough – even though it may contribute to the improvement of children's athletic and motor skills.

Long-term research and sports coaches' experience has shown that countries with more weekly hours of compulsory physical education at elementary school level have a healthier population. Healthy people are not sick as often and increase their country's competitiveness on the global market.

However, increasing the number of Phys Ed classes is not enough; one hour of playing dodgeball a week is not going to be much help. Phys Ed teachers need to teach students to stretch and strengthen their muscles, as well as offer them the chance to try out various sports. If a child finds a sport they particularly enjoy, they can continue doing it outside of school. Engaging in team sports improves a child's fitness and fosters team spirit and cooperation, which can serve them well in adulthood, both in their personal life and in their career.

Sleep is the last but definitely not the least important way to recharge physical energy. Unfortunately, many parents and children underestimate sleep's importance for their wellbeing.

People's need for sleep varies by age. Adults should sleep seven to eight hours a day; children need 8 to 16 hours of sleep a day, depending on their age. You will find the specific times for each age in the following table, which is based on recommendations provided by the American Sleep Association.[27]

CHILDREN'S NEED FOR SLEEP BY AGE

4 to 12 months of age	14–16 hours a day
1 to 2 years old	11–14 hours a day
3 to 5 years old	10–13 hours a day
6 to 12 years old	9–12 hours a day
13 to 18 years old	8–10 hours a day

Sleep is important for several reasons. When you perform an activity that you enjoy and that helps you get into flow state, your brain produces dopamine and oxytocin. To purge itself of these hormones, your brain needs sufficient sleep. Sleep deprivation leaves the brain partially flooded with hormones, which impairs your memory and concentration. Sleep is also crucial for the neuron myelination process. The brain requires sleep to form the appropriate synapses and myelinate them. Insufficient sleep prevents the brain from forming permanent synapses.

The quality of sleep is also affected by the time you fall asleep. Going to bed at 2am results in poorer quality of sleep than falling asleep before midnight. An hour of sleeping before midnight is worth two after.

EMOTIONAL ENERGY

Emotional energy is directly related to your mood and frame of mind. With your emotional energy at a sufficiently high level, you will stay happy and positive. Insufficient emotional energy results in irritation, grumpiness, and anxiety. Negative emotions drain both adults and children of energy – it is therefore essential for parents to cultivate their child's emotional intelligence. Once a child is aware of their emotions, they can start learning how to control them.

MENTAL ENERGY

Mental energy affects our ability to concentrate and deliver our best standard of performance even under stressful conditions. Maintaining focus is extremely difficult today. We are constantly flooded by information, messages, e-mails, and tasks. Smartphones and other digital technologies are grist to your Monkey's mill: the sheer volume of information can make your amygdala positively frantic. Millennia ago, when the amygdala developed, threats appeared in people's lives sporadically; today, something the Monkey interprets as a threat happens approximately every ten minutes. Your phone keeps ringing, texts keep beeping, your mailbox is full of important assignments. Back in Chapter 3, we discussed the pitfalls of linear thinking in an exponential world. Over a single week, your brain has to process as much information as your ancestors received throughout their entire lives.

The human brain is not prepared for the constant deluge of information and tasks. You need to restrict both your physical and mental access to digital devices and limit the time you spend multitasking in order to recharge your mental energy. The mindfulness technique described in this section is a great help in that. It helps you top up your mental energy levels and improves your perceptiveness.

SPIRITUAL ENERGY

THREE CIRCLES OF SPIRITUAL ENERGY

Spiritual energy is the strongest of the four types of energy that humans possess. It does not necessarily involve any kind of religious beliefs; the cornerstone of your spiritual energy is your mission in life. The sources of your spiritual energy form three symbolic circles, shown in the next figure. To give you a better understanding of what spiritual energy entails, we have used Jan's talents, activities, and values as an example.

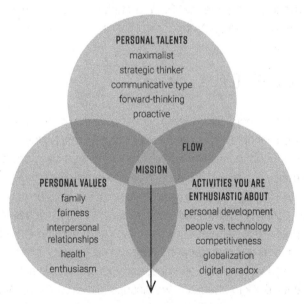

PERSONAL TALENTS
maximalist
strategic thinker
communicative type
forward-thinking
proactive

FLOW

MISSION

PERSONAL VALUES
family
fairness
interpersonal
relationships
health
enthusiasm

**ACTIVITIES YOU ARE
ENTHUSIASTIC ABOUT**
personal development
people vs. technology
competitiveness
globalization
digital paradox

PERSONAL MISSION / MEANING OF LIFE

The first circle contains the **talents** a person is born with.

The second circle involves the **activities** a person tries out from an early age, testing their innate talents. Activities that make the best use of your talents and that you enjoy help you get into flow state. Those are the activities a person chooses either for their career or hobby.

The third circle includes an individual's **personal values**. They represent the ideal standard of behavior for a person, both toward oneself and others. They provide a sort of inner code of conduct and should be one of the sources of your motivation. Everyone's personal values are a little different and can include such qualities as fairness, generosity, respect, sense of adventure, family, safety, openness, fun, and so on.

Personal values are formed from early childhood. Some theories claim that in every stage of life, a person is influenced by the five people closest to them. Those people can be the person's parents or loved ones but also favorite book or movie characters.

Jan: *The sense of fairness is one of my most important personal values. I once realized that my need for fairness stems from a young adult book I read as a boy. One of its protagonists became my own personal role model, and I followed his example of the need to treat everyone fairly.*

What makes personal values so important?

Some activities may get you into a flow state, but if you perform them while working for someone whose values are radically different from yours, they will not bring you a sense of fulfillment.

Suggestion: If you find it difficult to define your own personal values, think about the people in your life you admire, and try to identify what it is exactly that you admire them for. Those people can be your friends and loved ones but also famous and/ or important current or historical figures. Once you define the qualities you admire about them, you can embrace them as your

personal values. However, it is not enough to define your personal values: you also have to live by them.

Your own life's mission (or meaning of life) is in the intersection of the
three circles.

Suggestion: Draw the three circles on a piece of paper and fill
out your own talents, favorite activities, and personal values.

[22] Jan has developed this principle further into a concept he calls "Major League Thinking."

[23] You can find out more about the power of belief in Bruce Lipton's *The Biology of Belief – 10th Anniversary Edition* (2015), Hay House, UK.

[24] Source: Jan Mühlfeit, Melina Costi (2016). *The Positive Leader.* FT Press.

[25] The traditional approach toward education and career is geared toward fulfilling the lower levels of Maslow's pyramid. However, as you might have already guessed, people need to get all the way to the top of the pyramid to achieve happiness.

[26] Source: Steve, Peters (2012). *The Chimp Paradox: The Mind Management Programme to Help You Achieve Success, Confidence and Happiness*. Vermillion.

[27] https://www.sleepassociation.org/blog-post/much-sleep-children-need/

8

PARENT AS A POSITIVE COACH

Let's begin this chapter with a few words about the history of modern coaching. Coaching was a method first used by athletes; only later did it make its way to the business world and other areas, such as family therapy and education.

Timothy Gallwey is a former tennis coach and one of the founders of modern coaching. He has written a series of books which set forth a methodology he titled "the Inner Game," designed to help people develop personal and professional excellence in a variety of fields. Gallwey's seminal work is *The Inner Game of Tennis: The Classic Guide to the Mental Side of Peak Performance* (Random House, 1997). His later books (*The Inner Game of Work, The Inner Game of Stress, The Inner Game of Golf*, and several others) apply his training methods to other fields besides sports.

Jan: *Tim Gallwey's work has been a great source of inspiration for me. What I call "Major League Thinking" (becoming who you imagine you can be) is largely based on his concepts.*

Gallwey distinguishes between a person and their actions (who you are vs. what you do). This is actually a key concept in coaching.

Jan: *Imagine a child that has made a mistake (botched up a serve in tennis, for example). The coach/parent immediately starts scolding them: "You've messed up again. You're terrible. You'll never get it right!" The child's brain starts spinning up a story: "I'm a loser. I'll never learn to play tennis." This kind of internal monologue sends the child down a spiral of despair and anxiety. Unfortunately, many parents use this method when bringing up their children.*

Suggestion: Change your attitude. If you want your child to get better results, make sure they enjoy what they do. Find an activity they have an aptitude for and have fun doing.

Focusing on the child's activity, not their personality, does not attack their own sense of personal value and allows them to analyze their results without inferring anything about themselves as a person.

Gallwey once taught a journalist to play tennis in 40 minutes, using precisely this method – focusing on the game and gradually eliminating mistakes. His concept of "inner game" emphasizes the importance of a player's mental state on their success. Playing tennis, you can mentally replay your every bad shot and convince yourself you will never learn to play well. This sends you down a spiral of negative thoughts and failure. Or instead, you can tell yourself that you might have angled your racket badly on your last shot but your leg position was correct. This type of thinking leads to success. Coaching is about teaching you to think positively and constructively in order to improve.

COACH OR MENTOR?

A coach is a bit like a detective – except that instead of finding the perpetrator of a crime, they try to find the strengths and weaknesses of the person being coached, asking open-ended questions to get to know them better. People who ask closed-ended questions or tell their charge what to do are not coaches, they are mentors.

The following chart illustrates the difference between a coach and a mentor:

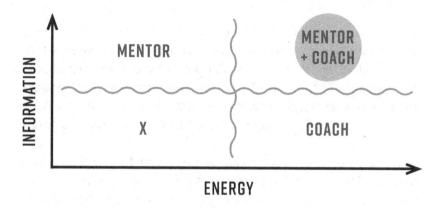

A **mentor** provides a great load of information based on their own experience. A mentoring session may not be especially stimulating and energizing, as the mentee needs to focus and actively listen to what is being said. Despite that, mentoring is an important skill.

A **coach** stimulates and energizes their clients. They do not judge or provide "tried and tested" solutions. A coach listens and asks open-ended questions that help the person being coached to find a solution on their own.

Coaching requires much greater participation from the person being coached than mentoring does. Being involved in the process of finding solutions will help the person being coached apply what they have learned in complicated situations. Comenius encouraged practicing this method with schoolchildren.

Jan: *As a student, I was thinking about my future career and decided to become a tennis coach. But then my father asked me: "I thought you liked working with computers. Are you sure this is what you want to do?" I'm certain that, had he simply told me to get a career in IT, I would have refused just to spite him, but he simply asked me a question; he never pushed me into anything. In the end, I changed my mind and went on to study information technology.*

Parents, teachers, trainers, and leaders should be both good mentors and coaches. They should both impart important knowledge (mentoring) and encourage healthy curiosity and the will to look for solutions (coaching).

As parents, you naturally share your experience and knowledge with your children. However, you should also try to coach them to think independently and innovatively and foster their natural inquisitiveness. In some situations, it is perfectly all right to simply tell your child: "That's the way *I* do it." In others, it's better to encourage the child to think creatively and try to find a solution on their own. This will not happen if you constantly tell the child what to do.

Some parents attending our workshops won't even let their child finish a sentence. They keep telling them how to solve things or what they did in the past and don't let the child think of their own answers and solutions.

Cyril Höschl: I know too many overprotective mothers who insist on accompanying their schizophrenic son to their appointments with me, even though the young man may be in his 20s or even 30s. If I had a mother like that, I would probably end up in a mental institution myself. I once asked one of my patients a question and his mother immediately started answering for him. "Have you had any interesting experiences lately?" I inquired. "Oh yes, he went to summer camp," his mother barged in. "Wait a minute; I wasn't asking you," I told her. "I was asking *him* because I want to know what *he* found interesting and important." Many mothers won't even let their child finish a sentence.

Suggestion: Your child does not need a spokesperson to answer every single question on their behalf. They need you to trust them and give them the space they need to find their own answers.

Coaching and mentoring are both important, but the two methods should always be applied separately.

Jan: *When I provide coaching to managers and CEOs, we usually set up some kind of goal. I start asking them questions and try to steer them toward the solution. Often, my clients will ask me for my take on the situation. At that moment, I let them know that we will be moving from coaching to mentoring. I try to give my clients more than one or two possible solutions because I would be putting them in a dilemma; I usually offer three options unless, of course, there is only one possible solution.*

WHAT TO FOCUS ON AS A COACH

Like the best coaches or leaders, a great parent focuses on the best in their child.[28] If you have more than one child, try to make them form a well-functioning team where each member will get plenty of inspiration.

Each coaching session should focus on the following points:

1. **Self-awareness**

2. **Defining a dream/goal**

3. **Creating a plan**

4. **Defining milestones on the path toward the dream/goal**

5. **Adjusting the path (if necessary)**

6. **Celebrating success / learning a lesson for the future**

You might not get it right from the start, but practice makes perfect. At the beginning, you will probably do more mentoring than coaching, but more and more often, you will have proud moments after you've managed to be patient and let your child find their own way instead of putting your own ideas in their head.

To get more experience, try to follow the ten rules of good coaching.

TEN RULES OF GOOD COACHING

1. **LISTEN ACTIVELY.** Focus on what your child says. It helps to listen to your child for about a minute and then briefly summarize what they said. You're showing them you've been paying attention.

2. **STAY POSITIVE.** You don't need to agree with anything your child tells you – simply be positive. That doesn't mean approving everything; even when you give critical feedback, try to use positive language and focus only on the subject at hand to let your child know you're not criticizing them as a person. It's important to express your trust in your child and hope for the future.

3. **BE OBJECTIVE.** Do not foist your own attitudes on your child. Ask open-ended questions. Praise your child for having done well, but don't ignore their mistakes. Constant praise is just as counterproductive as constant disapproval.

4. **BE PATIENT.** Don't rush your child. Keep asking questions. The greatest treasures often hide at the bottom of the pile.

Jan: *Whenever I feel like the coaching session is over, I tell myself that I already know enough, but then I always ask a couple more questions. I call it "the last drop."*

5. **BE FLEXIBLE.** Be prepared for the situation or your child's opinion to change. Coaching is not about showing the one and only right way but rather about showing a variety of options from which the person being coached can choose their own path.

6. **BE AVAILABLE.** When your child needs to discuss something with you, make it your priority to talk to them. Family is more important than anything else.

7. **BE OPEN.** Don't beat around the bush. Say things as they are.

8. **BE HONEST.** If you say one thing to your child but think another, they will lose their trust in you once they learn the truth.

9. **KEEP YOUR PROMISES.** Don't promise the impossible, but if you agree to something, you should keep your word.

10. **FOCUS ON STRENGTHS.** Don't focus overly on the things your child is not particularly good at. You can't turn an F into an A, but you can turn an A into an A+.

For better coaching, we recommend using a universal method applicable to both children and adults. It has been based on the well-known GROW model, developed by Sir John Whitmore, former British racing driver and pioneer of the executive coaching industry. Jan has adapted this model for his own needs and calls it U-GROW.

THE U-GROW MODEL

Each letter in the word U-GROW stands for a certain concept.

U – Uniqueness

G – Goal

R – Reality

O – Options

W – Way forward

Jan: *Throughout my years of coaching, I realized that even if you coach people properly, you might be steering them toward the wrong goal. Many top executives use coaching to move up the corporate ladder, but even though they earn more and more money, they become tired and disillusioned – not realizing that the ladder may not be leaning against the right wall. For this reason, I have adapted the GROW model to include the letter U, which stands for Uniqueness and expresses the fact that everyone is different and has different goals and needs. I consider uniqueness the starting point of any kind of coaching because it reflects the level of self-awareness of the person being coached. I help them to discover their talents, meaning of life, and sources of inspiration. Only then can we move toward their plans and motivation. Without the first step, their plans could be entirely misguided, and they could be following a path that won't actually bring them the sense of fulfillment they desire. That's why I find uniqueness so important.*

Here is how coaching using the U-GROW model works: At the start, talk to the child (adult) you're coaching about their talents and strengths. Follow by discussing the goals of the coaching sessions. Use open-ended questions to discuss the current situation of the person being coached and consider various options to achieve the desired goal. Finally, set up specific steps that will lead the child toward achieving their goal, and set a timeline for it.

To be able to put the U-GROW method into practice, try using the following model questions during your coaching sessions.

UNIQUENESS

WHO ARE YOU?

- Find out what makes you unique and what you see as the meaning of your life.

- What makes your child unique?

Possible questions to ask:

STRENGTHS

- What kinds of talents and skills do you think you have?

- What do other people say you are good at?

- How do you use your talents/skills?

- Which talents/skills do you like using most, and which do you use most often?

VALUES

- What do you think are the most important things for you? (e.g., friends, success, results, honesty, learning, family, etc.)

- When you are about to make an important decision, do you take your values into account?

ENTHUSIASM

- What do you enjoy the most? Which activities leave you energized? What are you the most enthusiastic about?

- Are there any activities that make you lose track of time?

GOALS / BENEFITS

- Is there anything these questions have made you realize?

G GOAL

WHAT WOULD YOU LIKE TO ACHIEVE?

- Define what the results of your child's effort should be.

- What are they trying to achieve?

Possible questions to ask:

- When you think about achieving this goal, what actually constitutes success?

- How are you/we going to measure your success?

- If you manage to accomplish your goal, how is it going to benefit you or others?

- What talents/strengths are you going to use to achieve your goal?

- When you think about achieving your goal, how enthusiastic do you feel about it? (The answer will reflect your child's energy and motivation, which are usually proportionate to their level of enthusiasm and the possibility to utilize their strengths.)

- How certain are you that you can accomplish this goal? (The answer indicates whether your child's skills or abilities are sufficient for this.)

- Does this goal belong among the things that are important for you? (Make sure the goal is in line with your child's values.)

- Is this goal in line with everything else in your life? (Child's school curriculum, hobbies, etc.)

REALITY

HAVE YOU MADE ANY PROGRESS SO FAR?

- Try to assess your child's current situation (their attitude, actions, and progress), their previous effort, and possible plans for the future.

Possible questions to ask:

- What have you already managed to accomplish on the way toward your final goal?

- What steps and actions have you already taken?

- Which talents/skills have you used?

- On a scale of 1 to 10, where 10 is the ideal outcome (achieving your goal), where do you think you are now?

- What would help you move forward?

- Are there any major problems or obstacles that could prevent you from achieving your goal?

OPTIONS

WHAT OPTIONS DO YOU HAVE?

- Help your child come up with possible ways of achieving their goal.

- Keep your own suggestions to a minimum. Ask open-ended questions. Let the child think about their options on their own.

- Which options do you see right now?

- What could you do next? (You can repeat different variations of this question to encourage your child to come up with more ideas.)

- What worked for you before?

- What do you think worked in similar situations?

- Which talents and/or strengths could you use for this kind of task?

- If you had unlimited resources (money, labor, etc.) at your disposal, what would you do with them?

- Who else could help you with this particular task?

- Would you like to hear some of my suggestions?

WAY FORWARD

WHAT NEXT?

- Help your child decide which steps/measures to take next. Create a detailed plan to boost your child's resolve.

- Offer various possible solutions to potential difficulties and promise your help and support if needed. Provide encouragement.

Possible questions to ask:

- Which of the options I've suggested would you like to try?

- What are you going to do? What is your first step going to be?

- Do you think this particular step will help you achieve your goal?

- Could you perhaps do even more?

- When are you going to start?

- How certain are you that you can do it?

- Are you looking forward to doing it?

- What are you going to do to stay motivated?

- Who else would you like to talk to or consult? Who else should know about your plans?

- What kind of support are you going to need from me?

- How often do you want to discuss your progress? (daily, weekly, monthly)

COACHING YOUR CHILD

Obviously, there's no need to coach your child to make simple decisions, like whether to get a yogurt or a sandwich for a snack. Coaching is suitable for situations when your child needs to make a crucial decision or discuss a serious problem.

Situations when coaching is useful:

- choosing a school;

- trouble with schoolmates;

- trouble with a teacher;

- choosing a sport/after-school activity;

- switching to a different sport/after-school activity;

- after a losing game / failed test;

- after a winning game / successfully completed test.

It is not only important to understand why your child has failed but also why they've succeeded. You shouldn't take your child's good results for granted.

Jan: *Steve Ballmer was Microsoft's CEO for 14 years. He was the one who asked me to join Microsoft's various international teams. As a young CEO of the Czech division of Microsoft, I went to meet him in Paris. It must have been back in 1998, at a time of government-ordered austerity measures, and the Czech economy was down by four percent. My team's profits were four million behind the plan mid-year. I knew why that had happened, however, and I explained the situation to Steve clearly. I finished by describing the steps we would take to meet our targets by the end of the year. The Hungarian CEO was next in line to report. His division had grown by 25 percent compared to the previous* *year and was currently 16 percent above the planned targets – but he still got sacked. To this day, I think it was because he couldn't actually sell his division's success properly.*

Coaching children is not easy, especially during adolescence – teens are prone to sulking and one-word answers rather than eloquent soul-searching.

> **Suggestion:** Don't get discouraged if things don't go the way you've envisioned. Start by taking small steps: ask a few tentative questions to let your child know you're giving them space to open up to you. Make sure they know they can tell you anything. They might not open up to you right away, but deep down they will know that whenever they get in a tight spot, they can talk to you.

MODEL SITUATION: PARENT COACHING A CHILD

A child comes home from school. She has failed a test.

Parent: Hey Teresa, what's up? How was school today?

Child: Okay, I guess...

Parent: So, nothing special?

Child: Well, kind of...

Parent: Okay, what happened?

Child: Well, we had classes as usual...

Parent: Did you have a test or something?

Child: Yeah, actually, we did. Math.

Parent: Okay, how did it go?

Child: It didn't.

Parent: I can see you're really sad and angry about it. I guess it must have been a tough test. Can you tell me how it went?

Child: I messed up. I studied for it, I really did, but I messed up anyway.

Parent: Well, that would annoy me too if I were you.

Child: Yeah. I hate that I studied so much but then just couldn't get anything right. I guess I panicked again.

Parent: Can you remember when exactly you started panicking?

Child: Yeah. It was during the first problem, or maybe the second...? When I tried to do the reverse check, it wouldn't come out right. I could do it last night when I studied for the test. The teacher wants us to do both the solution and the reverse check. I tried to do it over and over again and still couldn't get the right result. And then I ran out of time and didn't manage to solve the rest of the problems.

Parent: Why didn't you try to move on to a different problem?

Child: I wanted to finish that one since I'd already started it, didn't I?

Parent: How many problems were there altogether?

Child: I don't know... eight or nine... but I didn't really pay attention to the other ones.

Parent: How were points assigned for the problems? Was the first one the most important, or was the score divided equally?

Child: I don't know... equally, I guess.

Parent: So, if you were to take the test again now, would you do anything differently?

Child: I'm not sure... but yeah, maybe I would. Maybe I wouldn't panic so much and get stuck on that one problem. But if I can't solve it, what am I supposed to do? I have to finish it, right?

Parent: Why would you *have* to finish it? You said there were seven or eight other problems to solve.

Child: Yes, but I didn't even get to them.

Parent: You were too nervous, and the nerves wouldn't let you move on to another problem, right?

Child: Yeah. Everyone was working like crazy, and I got stuck at the first problem and I just knew I wouldn't be able to finish on time. The teacher kept telling us how much time we had left, that we only had this many minutes... And I knew there were at least seven other problems I had to solve and I wouldn't make it. And then I started panicking.

Parent: Okay, so let's sum this up. Perhaps it will help. You started doing the first problem, and it went just fine, didn't it?

Child: Yeah, I was doing all right.

Parent: So you were immersed in the moment, you were doing fine, and you weren't nervous at all?

Child: I *was* nervous. But just a bit.

Parent: And then you did the reverse check, right?

Child: Yeah.

Parent: But it didn't work. So you started panicking and thinking that you were failing the test.

Child: Yes. I panicked. The only thing I could think about was that I wasn't going to finish those other problems since I was still struggling with the first one and that I was going to get a poor grade.

Parent: So all you were thinking about was failing the entire test.

Child: Exactly. What would *you* have done?

Parent: Let me tell you what I think went on in your head, and then I'll explain how I would have dealt with it. Remember when we talked about the Monkey in your head? Well, that's what happened. It was the Monkey who took control.

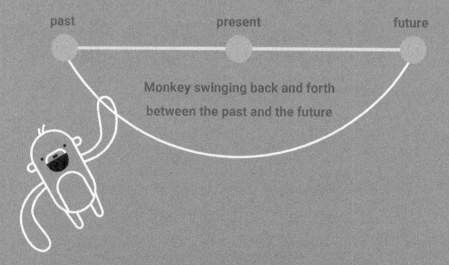

past   present   future

Monkey swinging back and forth
between the past and the future

When you messed up the reverse check, it was already in the past, over and done with. You should have returned to the present, as if you were just starting the test, and kept on working on each problem like it was the first one. Next time, why don't you just write off that one problem and move on to the next one?

Child: You mean I should just forget about it, even if I know I've done it wrong and I will get no points for it?

Parent: If those other problems have the same point value assigned to them, why not? If that one problem was worth 90 percent of the total score, and the rest were only worth ten percent put together, it would make sense to try and solve it, but you said that all the problems had the same point value. So, there's this one problem you just can't get right. The best way to ensure that you still get a decent grade is to start focusing again and return to the here and now. You can do that by moving on to the next problem. When you're solving a new problem, you're focusing on doing the math, on the present moment.

Child: But what should I do when I get so nervous? How do I calm down?

Parent: You get nervous because the Monkey in your mind gets stuck on the first problem. Next time something like that happens and you need to calm down, try to focus on your breathing. Then you can go back to the test.

Child: Easy for you to say. How do I tell that it's my Monkey that's giving me trouble? How do I know when to start breathing?

Parent: Can you try to describe how you felt when the reverse check wouldn't work? How could you tell you were nervous?

Child: Well... I kept biting the end of my pencil.

Parent: Were you breathing regularly?

Child: I don't know. I guess not. I trembled a little.

Parent: That was the Monkey, jumping around in your head. As soon as you can get your breathing back to normal again, the Monkey will calm down. It's like feeding it a banana so it stays still and happy. Do this four or five times – just breathe in, hold your breath, and then breathe out again. It won't take you more than 20 seconds to calm down and get back to work again. You can try chanting under your breath when you're doing it. "I'm giving... my Monkey... a banana."

Child: So I should just start breathing? Even though I'm running out of time?

Parent: Sure. You won't lose that much time by getting yourself to calm down, and then you can focus again. What do you think? Would that be worth a try?

Child: Weeeell... I guess I can try next time. Unless the teacher or the others distract me.

Parent: If you stay in the here and now, and focus on nothing but yourself and your breathing, nothing will distract you. You'll be 100 percent focused.

Child: So it really doesn't matter if I mess up some of the problems? You really think I should just move on?

Parent: Definitely. You might get one or two wrong, but you still have a chance to get the rest right. And even if you don't, we can still do something about it. You can learn from your mistakes. Next time, you'll know how to do it right and neither the math nor your Monkey will be able to throw you off balance.

It is standard practice for the teacher to announce how many minutes are left until the end of the test. They do this with good intentions, so that the student does not waste time and tries to finish as much of the test as they can; unfortunately, it is extremely stressful for most students. Children who have studied or practiced a lot will probably be able to stay focused even after they've been told how much time they have left, but most children are not like that. As a parent, try to explain to your child how important it is to have studied enough so that the correct solutions and information stay ingrained in their subconscious. It will help them to stay focused and not get distracted.

You should be aware, however, that even a positive emotion can disrupt your flow state.

~~~~~~

In 1993, tennis player **Jana Novotná** played in the final round of the Wimbledon tournament against Steffi Graf. She was 40 to 15 in the lead – but she still lost the game because she was prematurely over-joyed about winning. It only took five points – five perfectly executed present moments – for Graf to reverse the game.

~~~~~~

Pentathlete **David Svoboda** was just a step away from winning the Olympic gold but then got thrown off his horse, just as he was imagining himself standing on the winner's podium.

~~~~~~

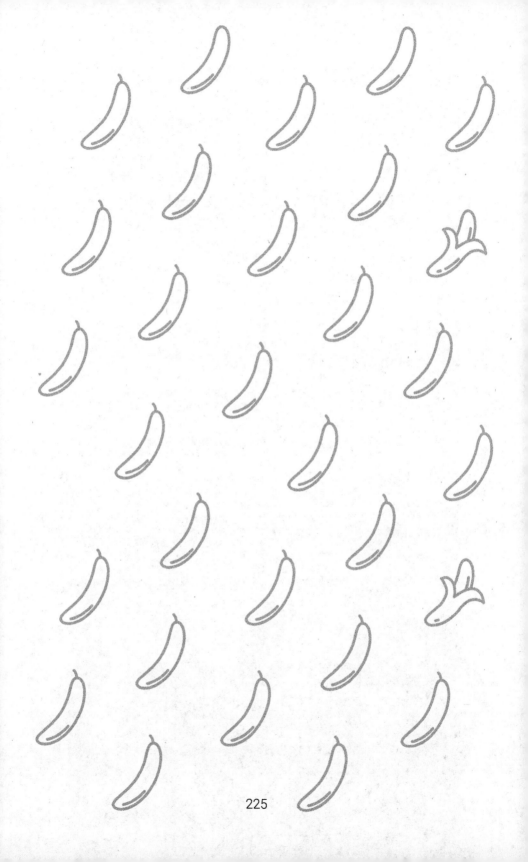

225

CONCLUSION

PREPARE YOUR CHILD FOR THEIR PATH IN LIFE, NOT A PATH FOR YOUR CHILD

The road to self-awareness is a long and hard one, but we believe that reading this book could make it a little easier for you. If it seems too hard or steep to your child, take their hand or take them in your arms; let them know you will always be there to support them. This book offers a wealth of information and advice that can help you guide your child, but never forget to listen to your heart and intuition as you go along.

Never forget that if you support your child in doing what they like best, they will have a chance to keep improving and retain that enthusiasm in the future.

Help your child become aware of how their mind works. Only then will they be able to start working on their self-improvement. All your child needs is time and your patience and help in discovering their talents and developing them into strengths. The digital age is extremely demanding and puts a lot of pressure on us. Help your child discover their strengths and weaknesses, the inner workings of their mind, and their likes and dislikes, so they can withstand the pressures and demands society puts on them.

Jan: *When my daughter graduated from a British high school in Prague, she received special awards in Mathematics, English, and German. Her schoolmates' parents kept asking me what we'd done to help her excel. I told them that, in all her years in high school, I'd never been to a single parent-teacher conference. I knew how hard she studied at home and saw no reason to go ask her teachers about her progress. I was convinced that if there had ever been a problem, her teachers would have let me know. I admit that I was probably a far better leader and manager than I was a father. But I believe that I managed to give my daughter an important example: when she saw how hard I worked on constantly improving myself, she tried to imitate me. It was leading by example at its best: behave the way you would like your child to act.*

Many top managers hiring new people for their team do not care about the applicants' education or school grades. Your past results are exactly that: your past. They say nothing about the way you think now or what experience you've gained. Don't despair if your child is not doing particularly well at school. As we've already explained, the standard education system encourages mediocrity rather than excellence. It's up to you as parents to help your child discover their talents and encourage their curiosity and desire to explore both the world and their own mind.

Jan: *At a lecture I recently gave at Harvard University, the students asked me how important I think it is to choose the right school. I told them that it doesn't matter where you study – what matters is where you're going to lecture one day. It doesn't matter where you start out, as long as you look far enough into the future. This is something you can help your child with.*

Kateřina: *If I let my lack of career experience or prestigious education discourage me, I would never have launched the parents-and-children project with Jan, and this book would probably never have come about. I always tell children and students that education can help them along the way, but it's not the be-all and end-all. You need to follow your dreams, talk about them, and try to make them come true – even if you might not make it on the first try.*

The feedback we regularly get from the many parents who have been to our workshops is ample proof that our method **works**. We even get feedback from the children themselves: a little girl who won her first tennis tournament, a boy who was the only one in his class to get an A on his math test, or a girl who started carrying a little plush monkey to school to help her remember what goes on inside her head when she gets stressed out.

Both our girls have profited enormously from your workshop. They try much harder in their riding classes, piano, and dance lessons. They remember what Jan told them: that success requires hard work. At school, they always try to remember about the Monkey, and they really like the nightly thankfulness ritual. They won't go to sleep unless we say thanks first. I can see how much self-confidence they've both gained. They trust in themselves and know how their mind works.

— David Pejchal

Thank you for the chance to attend your workshop. It's helped us take a step back and think about our priorities in life and realize that our children's personal growth is definitely one of them. We often think about the best way to prepare them for the challenges life will place before them, about the strengths and qualities we should help them develop, or which school to choose. Your workshop has helped us to find answers for many of our questions but has also raised a lot of new ones.

— Mr. and Mrs. Petruzel

You're doing a great job, and I hope that your methods and experience will one day help change our society, and especially the education system. Discovering our daughter's talents has reassured us about the path she should take in life. I love my job, and I hope that one day my daughter will love hers, too.

— Radka Havlíčková

Your workshop has helped both me and our boys to sort out the information in our heads and gain a much more optimistic outlook toward the future. Teenagers are not always easy to handle, but the workshop has given them just the right amount of information which they can now start to work with.

— Simona Šimonovská

Thank you for the chance to attend your workshop. Our son (11) has enjoyed it very much. I think it was important for him to understand what a talent actually is – that it's not just something that will win him gold medals or good grades but that it can involve such things as the ability to lighten up any situation, relieve others of stress, make and maintain friendships, or be a good organizer. We weren't hoping for him to discover some hidden "superskills" but rather to show him things he can appreciate about himself and that neither of us might actually have known about. And I think we have managed to do just that.

— Monika Fournial

Your workshop was great! I think my son (ten) has finally realized where his strengths really lie. He keeps going back to what he's learned, analyzing how his strengths work in particular situations. As he was leaving for school today, he told me that their teacher had gone crazy and announced two tests in one day but that he would remember to feed his Monkey and get through them.

— Michaela Radoušová

For the first time in his life, my son Simon (16, Asperger's syndrome) has managed to open up and overcome his fears and reservations, and he has asked whether he could actually come talk to you again. That has literally never happened before. You've done a great job. Thank you for the amazing time we had but mostly for showing Simon that it's up to him which direction his life is going to take.

— František Roučka

I would never have believed that your workshop could have such an impact on us and our self-awareness. I am especially grateful that you helped my son Ondrej (11) realize his inner strength. It was immediately obvious how happy, surprised, and excited he was about the things he heard and realized. He was able to stay focused and pay attention for the entire workshop, and he found virtually everything interesting. He couldn't stop talking about it afterwards. Thank you so much for having done such a great job with him. We have discovered and unlocked the things we were hoping to discover and unlock. All we need to do now is start helping him to manage his Monkey.

— **Libor Živný**

I was really looking forward to your workshop. I've watched some of your videos on YouTube, but obviously it's much better live. What I would never have expected was how much my son Kuba (17) would enjoy it. He kept talking about it for hours afterwards. It's not an easy thing to make a teenager so involved and interested! He passed his high school graduation exams shortly after the workshop, and he told me how much calmer and more focused he was.

— **Jaroslav Slánský**

Feedback like this is the exact reason why we do our workshops. They are both our life's mission and a source of great fulfillment. It is the happy parents and children who give us the strength and energy to go on and keep improving. Our workshops are a work of love, based on our firm belief that everyone has the right to live a full, genuine life, utilizing their own potential to the fullest.

Don't try to imitate anyone. Be yourself. Everyone has a unique set of talents and strengths. Focus on what you are good at, not what your colleagues or schoolmates can do better.

As parents, encourage your children to be themselves — the best version of themselves. The only way to live your life the best way you can is to be yourself.

YOU WERE BORN AN ORIGINAL. DON'T LIVE YOUR LIFE AS SOMEONE ELSE'S COPY.

The world is full of imitators, but it's the genuine, original, unique people who make history. We wish both you and your children the best of luck in your endeavor to achieve true self-awareness.

— Kateřina & Jan

ACKNOWLEDGMENTS

We would like to express our heartfelt thanks and gratitude to all those who have made the writing of this book possible.

First and foremost, we would like to thank our loving parents and wonderful families who have given us their unconditional support and understanding. We have learned so much from them and still have more to learn.

We will always be thankful to one of our greatest teachers and sources of inspiration, John Amos Comenius, whose "school by play" concept has inspired our own vision. We are also grateful to a number of other great educators, thinkers, scientists, psychologists, and experts in the field of positive psychology, personal development, education, and working with children and families.

Our thanks also go to Petra Kryštofová, our amazing editor, who has brought order to our chaos, given this book a proper form, and made it far more readable (and all that while carrying twins, who therefore also deserve our thanks for their patience). We would also like to thank our graphic editors for making this book so beautiful and playful in form: Přemek Zajíček, for designing the cover, and Ema Pavlovská, for her illustrations and overall visual concept. Many thanks also to Monika Součková for her patience in transcribing our recorded thoughts into a coherent text. Many thanks also go to Lucie Mikolajková, the book's translator from Czech to English.

We would also like to thank all those who have contributed their knowledge and experience to make this book even better: Cyril Höschl, Dagmar Svobodová, and Jaroslav Svěcený. We are also grateful to all those who have given us their kind words of support: Terezie Tománková, Denisa Rosolová, Veronika Kašáková, Radek Ptáček, and Marian Jelínek.

Many thanks to our entire team for their excellent work in helping organize our workshops and other activities.

Special thanks belong to all the parents, children, students, and teachers who collaborate with us frequently and to all those who attend our courses, lectures, and workshops. You are all a great inspiration to us.

And last but not least, our thanks go to all those mothers and fathers and everyone who is currently reading this book in an effort to set out on the path toward self-awareness. Thank you for your time, enthusiasm, and desire to both learn and help your children to develop all aspects of their personalities.

Kateřina: *I also have to thank Bubbles, my four-legged friend, who has taught me so much about staying in the here and now, who showers me with love every day, and shares that love with all the children we meet.*

Thank you!

— **Kateřina & Jan**

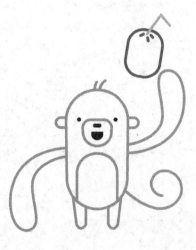

Part 3

BONUS INTERVIEWS

Cyril Höschl, psychiatrist
Jaroslav Svěcený, virtuoso violinist
Dagmar Svobodová, mother of three sons

INTERVIEW WITH PSYCHIATRIST CYRIL HÖSCHL

(ON HIS CHILDHOOD, HIS FOUR CHILDREN, AND THEIR TALENTS)

Cyril Höschl is a prominent Czech psychiatrist. In an interview given exclusively for this book, he talks about the influence of a person's genetic makeup on their character, nature versus nurture, and the role of chance in combining the various factors determining a person's path in life, illustrating the mystery of developmental psychology through his own example and that of his four children.

WHAT WAS YOUR OWN CHILDHOOD LIKE?

It's hard to recall one's childhood in an unbiased manner. Adults interpret their own childhood differently than when they were actually children. My early childhood was largely influenced by the fact that we used to live in a fairly secluded place. My parents had to leave Prague and move to the small town of Jevany. Before World War II, Jevany was sort of a summer resort for rich city people, but around the time we moved in, hardly anyone lived there during the winter. From October through May, everyone left for the city and there were only a few permanent residents left. I had no friends at all; I played alone in a huge garden full of pine and fir trees. My brother was born when I was five years old, and two years later we moved again to Liberec, a city in the north of Bohemia.

My mother had a hard time keeping the house; with no public transportation, she had to walk nearly a mile to the nearest store. Coal was rationed, and she had to make do with what we were given, even if it was freezing outside. My father commuted to work in a large engineering plant. There was no time or opportunity for the kind of things today's parents routinely provide for their children. We had no television, just an old crackling radio. I used to spend a lot of time outside. I hardly ever saw my father – he came home late at night and left early in the morning. Sometimes he would go and bathe in the nearby pond after work, and that was pretty much the only time I would see him. For part of my early childhood, he was conscripted to compulsory military service and left home altogether.

All of that changed when we moved to Liberec. We spent a lot more time together. I started school and found new friends. My memories from that time are much clearer. From today's perspective, my parents were perhaps a little too strict. We had regular bedtimes and mealtimes; our life was very structured and ordered. My parents were not overly demonstrative in their feelings, but they were by no means cruel. They were not religious fanatics or anything of the sort. They simply believed in the principles coined by education specialists at the time, which emphasized a strict regime – washing your hands before meals, taking naps even if the child is not sleepy... things like that. But there were no physical punishments, so, looking back at it, I actually think my parents were pretty liberal.

As my brother and I got older, we started rebelling against some of those rules, although there were others that we adopted over time and even embraced, which meant the pressure from our parents decreased. I remember this one rule my parents had: we always had to dry ourselves off completely when we came out of the bath – because if we didn't, we would get eczema, we were told. As a physician, I am now aware that it was most likely nonsense, but I was so brainwashed by my parents that, even as an adult, I would always try to dry myself off as much as I could. However, overall I would say that I had a fairly liberal upbringing.

As far as my parents were concerned, my mother was the one who kept the family and household going, while my father was more of an intellectual role model for me. He was good at math, he spoke five languages, and he could recite poetry by heart. He was very introverted and not especially communicative, but children have a great ability to sense both genuineness and falseness in people. My dad had a natural authority; my brother and I admired him a lot. He could be extremely tenacious and persistent in handling problems – he would not stop until he found a solution. One of my sons inherited this strong-willed attitude from him.

WHY ONLY ONE OF YOUR SONS?

"Nature vs. nurture" is a question that natural science has been trying to answer for ages. Countless experiments and research programs have been devoted to it. There is an old book by Helen Grace Carlisle, **Mothers Cry**, first published in 1929. It tells of a simple, poor mother of several children. One of her sons was a successful architect; one of her daughters was killed – and another of her sons was the killer. Three children carrying the same set of genes, brought up by the same mother in the same environment, and their fates ended up being completely different. If the parents' genetic information was the only determining factor, they would all have been very similar; and, conversely, if environment was the crucial factor in a child's development, three individuals brought up in the same environment would have developed similar personalities. However, genetic variations are endless, just as the environmental factors are, and the resulting combination ensures that no two individuals turn out exactly the same. Genetic traits may also skip a generation, so a son may take more after his grandfather than his father.

I always admired my father's neutral, almost indifferent attitude toward money. He'd never earned a particularly high salary – he made enough to live moderately well, but he never cared about making a lot of money. He was not much of a spendthrift, either. From today's perspective, he was almost an ascetic. I never saw him drink alcohol, and he ate very modestly. It was completely natural for him to live this way; there wasn't any kind of ideology behind it. I used to wonder whether he ever "spoiled" or rewarded himself by anything – and I came to the conclusion that solving applied mathematical problems was sort of an intellectual reward and actual fun for him. We used to go on a lot of hiking trips, which was also kind of typical: hiking is an ascetic sport that does not require spending a lot of money. Father liked swimming and cycling, but had he had to buy an expensive bike to be able to ride, he wouldn't have done it. He didn't care what he wore – my mother would buy all his clothes for him, and he would wear them until they fell apart. Personally, I like the occasional self-indulgence. I enjoy good food and drink, but I don't care much about luxuries. In that, I've always followed my father's example. Sometimes I realize that my occasional hedonism is a sort of a substitute for my father's intellectual pursuits.

HAVE YOUR CHILDREN INHERITED ANYTHING FROM THEIR GRANDPARENTS?

My wife is an artist, and some of our children have inherited her artistic inclinations. We have four children together, two sons and two daughters, and every one of them is an absolute original. They all prove that the nature-vs.-nurture relationship is extremely complicated and influenced by countless factors and their various constellations.

My oldest daughter, Karolina, is a lot like my mother, both physically and mentally. She's a very talented linguist. She speaks five different languages and has three college degrees. She graduated from a police academy, then got a degree in translating and interpreting and earned a PhD in media and communication at the college of social sciences. She used to teach languages, and then she focused on becoming a mother. She has six children now. She has a tendency to underestimate herself. I once asked her why she had studied so much if all she does now is take care of her children. "Well, what was I supposed to do before I had children?" she said. "Sit at home and do nothing?"

My youngest daughter, Kristina, is completely different. She's very athletic and muscled. She loves adventure and adrenaline-fueled activities. She works as a paramedic, either in an ambulance van or a medical helicopter. She often finds herself in dramatic situations: she's saved skiers in the Alps, been to Afghanistan with Doctors Without Borders, climbed Mount Everest, and parachuted from an airplane. Situations like that require quick thinking and snap decisions; there's no time for sentiment or long-winded contemplation. You have to make the right decision without thinking about it, which requires a great deal of mental resilience. She often works in terrible conditions, performing difficult medical interventions out in the open – on the road, in storms and mud, surrounded by curious bystanders. I once asked her if she felt stressed out. She told me she had two options. She could either do nothing and the person would die, or she could do something and the patient may still die but might not. She's giving them a chance. A bad thing has already happened to them, so whatever she does will only improve their situation. She has a soldier's sense of discipline. When I call her, she always asks me whether I'm calling about something important. If I tell her no, that I just want to talk, she simply hangs up. She's the one who decides when we will meet again and when she can make time for me. She's extremely efficient, both at work and in her personal life.

My son Cyril, who's now 36 years old, has always been a problem solver, even as a little boy. Swiss developmental psychologist Jean Piaget postulated that thinking was internalized behavior. A small child first acts, then thinks. What happens to the vase on the table if I pull down the tablecloth? The child has to actually pull down the cloth to be able to imagine the outcome. The ability to imagine possible consequences only comes with experience. That's why you need to watch over small children constantly – they act before thinking. The cognitive process can therefore be described as internalized behavior. Actual motor acts start happening symbolically in the child's mind. As a child, my son was always tinkering with something. He had incredible mechanical skills. A friend of mine had this old, broken barometer at home. He felt it would be a shame to just throw it away so he brought it to Cyril, so he could try to fix it. Cyril had barely started going to school, and I thought there was no way he could fix that thing. But he simply wouldn't give up – just like his grandpa. He researched everything about barometers, then he shut himself in his room, and the next day he brought me the barometer – all fixed and working again. I think I gave him an orange as a reward or something like that. It was then that I realized that not only was he a talented mechanic but that when he got his hands on a problem, he wouldn't stop until he solved it.

When Cyril was about 12 years old, I bought a laser printer. He wanted to print something on a plastic sheet, but he used a sheet that was not heat resistant. It got stuck all around the cylinder. I yelled at him, telling him that the printer was all broken and I would simply have to throw it away. He just started sniveling, and then he told me he could try to fix it. You can't fix it, I told him, there's nothing you can do. But he begged me to let him try before I actually threw the printer away. He took the printer to his room and took it completely apart. He pulled out the cylinder and, using a razor blade and a pair of tweezers, he scraped away all that melted plastic, piece by tiny piece. I didn't believe he could put the printer back together, but he did. I still have it today, and it still works. You can't even buy parts for it anymore, but I keep it for sentimental reasons. So why did I talk about thinking as internalized behavior? It was because Cyril had actually transformed this ability to manipulate the world with his hands into an ability to manipulate the world in his mind and became a software engineer. Today, he's mostly too lazy to do manual work himself, but he's never lost the skills. The other day, he had workmen in his apartment to build some kind of a partition. They kept telling him it wasn't possible to do it exactly the way he wanted to, so he bought a drill and fixed the partition himself – better than a professional joiner could have done. The only reason why he's never turned these skills into a career is that he finds creating software more challenging.

Our youngest son, Patrik, has inherited his mother's artistic skills. He's had a lot of success with his graphic designs, but that's not really what he wants to do. He studied script writing at a film academy. After graduation, he moved to London and started a company with a friend of his. They create games for mobile phones. Patrik designs the game rules, the back story, and all the game levels. He knows exactly what to do to make the game attractive. He designs and animates all the characters, and his friend then writes the code to make it work both on iPhones and Android phones. Their company, Hexage Limited, has made it onto the list of top mobile phone game producers in the world. Patrik met his wife when he was still in the film academy. She is from Poland and works as a screenwriter. They speak Czech together, and their children speak both Czech and Polish.

The point I'm trying to make is that our children grew up in the same environment and were born to the same parents, and yet every one of them is completely unique. Cyril has always been very money-oriented. He started making money designing software when he was 12 years old. I actually used to borrow money from him sometimes. He was not old enough to have his own bank account, so he had to use his older sister as a front. One day he came to me complaining that I gave his brother Patrik CZK 3.60 for a school notebook. "Aren't you ashamed?" I told him. "You're earning your own money. Why would you envy your brother a few korunas for a notebook?" His answer was very typical of him. "So, just to make it clear," he said, "is being able to make my own money actually a bad thing? You want to punish me for it by not giving me money anymore? You're going to pay for my brother's school stuff, but not for mine? Is making money a crime? Should I start buying my own food from now on? I just want you to explain it to me." I had no choice but to back off and give him the money. My oldest daughter, Karolina, complained that we had spoiled him. I told her that we treated him just the same as we did her. So, when someone's child does – or does not – turn out the way their parents wanted them to, who's to blame? The parents?

HOW DO YOU SEE YOUR CHILDREN'S CHILDHOOD AND THE WAY YOU TREATED THEM?

I think that our children had a great childhood – but then again, children usually perceive things differently than their parents. We were very liberal parents. When the kids got older, I didn't even know which school they went to. I think I went to a parent-teacher conference exactly once;

my wife sent me. Too bad I didn't even know which of the children I was there for. Helping them do their homework or helping them choose which college to go to? I never did that. That was more my wife's thing. Actually, I have a pretty controversial opinion about that: I think it doesn't really matter where and what you study. Either you're good at something or you're not, and no amount of studying is going to change that. You have to want to learn for your own sake. I don't believe in elite schools. If I ever need my gallbladder removed, I will simply go to a regular hospital. The nurses might be grumpy, there might be cocoa spilled on the floor, but the doctors there perform hundreds of these surgeries every year, so I can be fairly sure they're not going to kill me. In a super-special private hospital, they could be doing no more than three such surgeries a year. I'd think I was getting the best care available, but it might not be true at all.

LOOKING BACK TODAY, IS THERE ANYTHING YOU WOULD HAVE DONE DIFFERENTLY?

I think it was a good decision to let my children fend for themselves, rather than always paving the way for them. I wouldn't change anything.

I think it's best to allow children to learn to take care of themselves. "I'm not going to give you bread – I'm going to teach you how to bake it," is my motto. With young children, up until the age of 15, perhaps even 18, you obviously try to protect them against any unfair treatment, help them when they're in any kind of pain (whether emotional or physical), and care for them when they're ill. However, I am firmly against smoothing the way for them or giving them an unfair advantage. My daughter Karolina tried to get into medical school but failed the entrance exams. I was Dean of the Faculty of Medicine at the time, but I did not try to help her in any way. She failed the test; she didn't get in. Tough luck.

We're not social engineers. You never know what turns out to be the right choice. I have no way of knowing whether one of my children's paths will lead them somewhere where they will be much happier than if they had studied at an elite private school their daddy had chosen for them. If you put yourself into a godlike position as a parent and start bending reality to your will, mistakes will start piling up.

I know too many overprotective mothers who insist on accompanying their schizophrenic sons to their appointments with me, even though the young man in question may be in his 20s or even 30s. If I had a mother like that, I would probably end up in a mental institution myself. I once asked one of my patients a question and his mother immediately started answering for him. "Have you had any interesting experiences lately?" I inquired. "Oh yes, he went to summer camp," his mother barged in. "Wait a minute; I wasn't asking you," I told her. "I was asking *him* because I want to know what *he* found interesting and important." Many mothers won't even let their child finish a sentence.

Jan: *One of the reasons I ended up in a mental institution briefly was the fact that my mother was a perfectionist. It was taken for granted that I would get straight As at school. Whenever I got an A minus, my mother would start asking: "What do you mean, A minus? How could you not get an A?"*

When I got my first corporate job, I thought that being the best was great – but being second best actually meant being the first among losers. I focused entirely on performance. Giving myself a mental rest meant losing. Eventually, it all spiraled out of control.

WHO WAS THE MORE HANDS-ON PARENT, YOUR WIFE OR YOURSELF?

My wife definitely spent a lot more time with the kids. She was also the more anxious parent, always worrying that they would fall down, catch a cold, get injured... so I tried to balance it out and let them run free. I first took them rappelling when they were around five to seven years old. My daughter Kristina recently gave an interview about her hobby, mountain climbing. She said her love of climbing went all the way back to when she was a little girl, when I took her to the mountains and let her rappel down a rock. My other children took it as a great adventure, but that was it. For Kristina, the adrenaline rush she got from it resulted in a lifelong passion for climbing. Today, abseiling down a rope from a helicopter is a part of her daily job.

WHEN DID YOU DECIDE TO SPECIALIZE IN PSYCHIATRY?

I liked a lot of things when I was young. I think the thing I wanted most was to become a film director, but to get into film school, you had to pass a talent exam, presenting a portfolio of your photos. I was lazy and slow in putting it together and didn't manage to do it on time. My mother wanted me to become a doctor. I applied for medical school but also for the faculty of arts, where I wanted to major in psychology, and I even applied for the school of engineering in Liberec. I didn't much care about the school itself, but it meant staying at home. When I went to check my results after the entrance exam to medical school, I realized I'd been accepted, so I didn't even try for the other two schools. I told myself that a degree in medicine was sort of an all-round education, kind of like high school. After graduation, I had a hard time finding a position until an acquaintance of mine told me that the Psychiatric Research Institute had two openings, so I applied, together with a friend who'd graduated in the same year as I did. The interview was conducted by Professor Hanzlíček, director of the institute. He was very open about everything, including politics, which was quite unusual at the time. He asked me whether I'd considered specializing in psychiatry before, and I told him I hadn't, that I'd simply heard they had a position open. I thought I'd completely blown my chances, but the Professor simply told me I'd be starting in September. He must have seen my surprise. "You see," he told me, "I have candidates lining up who think becoming a psychiatrist will help them solve their own problems – but I really need someone normal."

I'd read some of Freud's treatises back in college but only to expand my general knowledge. I would never have thought I would actually specialize in psychiatry. I agreed to stay for a year, and then, if a position opened somewhere else, I would transfer. But there were no openings after that first year, and I'd actually started enjoying my job. After I got board certified, I decided I would stay. If I had to make the same choice today, I would choose psychiatry in a heartbeat.

TODAY'S CHILDREN ARE OFTEN EXPECTED TO HAVE A CLEAR VISION OF THEIR FUTURE CAREER BEFORE THEY EVEN APPLY TO COLLEGE. WHAT'S YOUR OPINION ON THAT?

There are two types of people: first, there are those with a very specific talent who realize very early in life that there's really only one thing they want to do. They have no choice but to do what they were made for. The second group of people includes more rounded individuals, who may have to do a bit of trying and soul-searching to actually find out what they want to do. Some chance encounter might inspire them to choose a career path that will lead to a sense of fulfillment.

INTERVIEW WITH JAROSLAV SVĚCENÝ, VIRTUOSO VIOLINIST

(ON HIS TALENTS AND HIS TWO DAUGHTERS)

WHAT WAS YOUR CHILDHOOD LIKE? HOW DID YOUR PARENTS HELP YOU DEVELOP YOUR PERSONALITY AND YOUR TALENT?

I started playing the violin when I was about five-and-a-half years old. It was actually my grandfather who'd steered me toward music: he was a violinist, bandmaster, and music teacher. He gave music lessons at home, so I saw how it all worked. My mother was a high school teacher and a choir master, so I was immersed in music from my early childhood. One day, grandpa simply put a violin in my hands and told me to try. I'd always admired my grandfather's organizational skills and his ability to be creative. I inherited some of that from him. Grandpa soon realized he couldn't teach me himself and signed me up for music classes. I started out with my new teacher when I was six years old, and grandpa simply supervised me from a distance. Soon I started playing in front of an audience. The principal of my elementary school decided I would represent the school by playing at public events. I would sit in class, and the school PA system would sound: "Student Jaroslav Svěcený to the principal's office, please!" The principal always told me what a great asset I was for the school, and how proud he was of me, and then sent me to play somewhere. I played at virtually all the local cultural and social events. Once I even played at the local train station! It was a great way to get used to playing in public and lose my stage fright.

DID YOU WANT TO PLAY ANY OTHER INSTRUMENT AS A CHILD?

Considering that I pretty much grew up hearing the violin played every day, it was a done deal. I studied piano as my second instrument, but I never enjoyed it much. I knew I had to learn it as my secondary instrument, but my heart was never in it. The violin, on the other hand, simply fascinated me. I've always loved its shape, and I particularly love the smell. When I first went to a violin maker's workshop, I fell in love with the smell of propolis and natural resin. All those brand new, beautifully fragrant violins... I thought I was in heaven! So this is how my love for the violin actually started, from the smell. At my concerts, I like to say that I was just a little violin junkie.

AS A YOUNG BOY, DID YOU EVER GET STAGE FRIGHT?

Of course I did. Especially at the beginning. Playing a solo violin requires a specific mindset. I've always been a good public speaker, though, and it helped me set the mood at my concerts.

WHO DID YOU INHERIT YOUR RHETORICAL SKILLS FROM? YOUR MOTHER?

As a high school teacher and college professor, speaking in public was a natural part of my mother's job. I guess I do take after her in that respect. I've always liked presenting my own concerts.

SO YOU BOTH PLAYED AT AND PRESENTED YOUR OWN CONCERTS? HOW OLD WERE YOU WHEN YOU STARTED?

I must have been 11 or 12 years old. Talking to the audience calmed me down and helped me segue naturally into playing. Some musicians are not able to say a single word, though; they would only get nervous and thrown off.

HOW BIG AN AUDIENCE DID YOU USUALLY PLAY FOR?

It varied. Sometimes I played for 30 people; sometimes, for 500.

DID YOU PLAY FOR CHILDREN OR ADULTS?

Both. It was a lot more difficult to play for children because children are much harder to entertain. If you don't catch their attention, they'll just keep chattering among themselves. I realized I had to make some kind of introductory speech. Had I just started playing Bach, whom they'd never heard of, they would simply not have listened to me. They had no interest in classical music. I had to explain the music to them, make it more accessible.

Talking to the audience helped me to set a certain mood for my music. It doesn't always work that way, but I always felt better if I could establish some kind of rapport with my audience besides eye contact and the music.

SO YOU'VE ACTUALLY COMBINED TWO OF YOUR TALENTS – MUSICAL AND COMMUNICATION SKILLS.

I've always needed to put my audience in a receptive mood. Talking to them helped me do that. Only then did I tune the violin and start playing.

WHEN YOU TOOK THE TALENT TEST, IT TURNED OUT YOU WERE BEST AT HELPING PEOPLE IMPROVE AND DEVELOP.

Your concerts are both educational and entertaining: you tell your audience about history, the making of violins, and so on...

You must have learned to link this talent to your sense of empathy quite early on.

I guess so. I've never been one for staid, conservative musical performances. I've always wanted my concerts to be different. I hate it when classical music is presented as something exclusive. Back when classical music first emerged, it was not reserved for the elite. Bricklayers would whistle the tune of Mozart's *A Little Night Music* while working because it was simple and catchy. "See?" I always tell my audience. "It's just a G chord taken apart!" A simple theme can become beautiful and timeless if it's well written. Mozart's music is a work of genius precisely because, at its heart, it's extremely simple. The brilliance of the old masters never fails to fascinate me. I've always wondered how it was possible for Mozart to have written so many compositions over a mere 35 years. He must have had them all in his head, finished and ready to put down on paper. He couldn't have created them slowly as he went along.

I've always wanted my peers, and young people in general, to understand that classical music is actually the pop music of the past. It was once as hip as the greatest rock or pop hits. The classics – Vivaldi, Bach, Mozart – don't really require any explanation, but I want to tell people about them because many of them have never heard them before. A lot of people know absolutely nothing about classical music.

SCHOOL PROVIDES CHILDREN WITH A LOT OF INFORMATION BUT TAKEN COMPLETELY OUT OF CONTEXT, WHICH MAKES IT HARDER TO REMEMBER.

One of our teachers once told us about Tchaikovsky and the way he wrote his famous Capriccio. His hotel stood opposite the local military barracks, and he drew inspiration from the sounds he heard from there. I remembered this because it was an interesting tidbit, and once it actually helped me win a trivia quiz. Had the teacher simply played the music, without any kind of background information, I would never have remembered it.

I think that well-structured and well-taught music classes are essential in elementary school. They should be taught by teachers who really like music, who don't just deliver dry lectures. One of my music teachers was a musician himself. He would give us instruments in class to play. "You could try this," he would say. "It was composed by So-and-so. And you know how he came to write it?" He would explain the context to us, and we all loved it. I suppose what I'm trying to say is that to learn, you need motivation – an incentive to learn something you've never heard of before. If you don't explain classical music to people in an engaging, interesting way, it will seem too difficult and inaccessible to them.

I've always wanted to bring music closer to the people. I've never accepted that classical music was only for a select few. My key motivation is to tell people about music. When I stand in front of a packed auditorium, I feel like what I'm doing is meaningful and that the rapport I've always tried to establish with my audience has paid off. I used to think that once I got older, I would no longer have to do these popularization programs – but quite the contrary, they're more necessary now than ever. In today's fast-paced society, people are often unable to connect with or understand anything deeper.

YOU'RE GIVING PEOPLE A SORT OF SAFE PLACE. PEOPLE EITHER LIVE IN THE PAST OR THE FUTURE; VERY FEW ARE FULLY IMMERSED IN THE PRESENT.

That's actually why I started my classical music club some 12 years ago. I realized that for the people who came there, it was sort of like a haven of peace, of music, as well as a source of interesting knowledge. The peacefulness was in stark contrast with today's fast-paced lifestyle. Technology has made everything faster but also more shallow – and those who are not happy about that are looking for safe havens like a classical music club. Over the two hours we spend together during each session, I can see their faces changing, as if they've shed their fatigue and the ever-present inner stress. Suddenly, they can let go. It's beautiful, watching people for whom music is a way to relax. It's like giving them an energy boost, like a spa weekend packed into a couple of hours. A lot of people have trouble relaxing these days. I can see how tense they are, how harried. They always think about the tasks and duties ahead of them. It forces them to live in the future, instead of the present moment, which is really not good for their general health. It seems that music can function as a sort of cure – and one without any harmful side effects at that.

I THINK IT'S BECAUSE WHEN YOU LISTEN TO MUSIC, YOU CAN JUST BE. AND WHEN YOU DO THAT, YOU ARE IN THE HERE AND NOW. WHEN YOU'RE CONSTANTLY WORKING OR THINKING, YOU'RE LIVING IN THE FUTURE.

By living at such a fast pace, we've stopped thinking about things properly. We are always restless and stressed out. I'm sure you've noticed, and a lot of people have a hard time concentrating these days.

DO YOU REMEMBER THE FIRST TIME YOU ACTUALLY GOT INTO A FLOW STATE WHEN PLAYING THE VIOLIN?

It came quite late – I think it was around the time I was at the music academy. I must have been over 20 years old already. I could get into flow while playing pieces I'd practiced really long and hard and that I'd played for an audience many times. It was a very interesting experience, which I've since had several times in the course of my career: as I was playing, I felt as if I'd stepped outside myself and watched myself playing. I was unbelievably happy. It was as if I had no control over my hands or the bow; I was playing on autopilot and yet it wasn't routine. It's hard to describe. I told a few people about it, but they must all have thought I was bonkers.

THAT'S ACTUALLY SOMETHING SIMILAR TO WHAT TOP SURGEONS DESCRIBE HAPPENING TO THEM DURING OPERATIONS.

I really felt it. I saw myself playing, and as the piece came to an end, I simply slipped back inside my own body, and then it was over. It was the pinnacle of what I could ever hope to achieve: an unbelievable feeling of pure happiness which can last several minutes. You're completely aware of yourself, and you're going through something completely indescribable. It completely threw me. What is it in our mind and soul that allows us to experience something like that? It goes against rational thinking, and most pragmatic people will not understand, but it's real. And then there's another unbelievable feeling that goes with that – when I feel the audience getting there with me.

IT'S BECAUSE EMPATHY IS ONE OF YOUR TALENTS. YOU CAN TELL WHEN THE AUDIENCE IS COMPLETELY CAPTIVATED.

I am a very open, communicative person. People often tell me: "I didn't even think you noticed us. You had your eyes closed all the time!" The opposite is true, in fact. When I close my eyes, I communicate with the audience on a whole different level. It's my way of talking to them. And when I realize they're receptive, they're reacting to me, I'll play my heart out because that's exactly what I've been waiting for. That's why I do what I do. If someone banned me from performing in public, I'd put down the violin and never play again.

DO YOU ACTUALLY KNOW WHY YOU TEND TO CLOSE YOUR EYES?

It's your subconscious at work. If you keep your eyes open, you might glance in the direction of a listener who's not paying attention. Your

Monkey would immediately latch on to this and start telling you that maybe you're not as good as you thought. When you close your eyes, though, you can avoid this and still feel the audience, thanks to your sense of empathy.

People have asked me many times which country I prefer to play in. I keep telling them it doesn't matter to me. What matters is the chemistry in the concert hall at the exact moment I'm playing. I don't care whether it's in Germany, Turkey, or Indonesia. Chemistry is the key. When that works, when everyone gets into the spirit, when we talk about music and when we all feel it, it all turns out great. It's all about harmony.

There are so many excellent musicians all over the world; you have a hundred great violinists or pianists on every corner. The important thing is to make people want to come and listen to you again, not because you have flawless technique or unbelievable speed but because you put something of yourself into the music. That's why people want to hear you again — because of the humanity you put into your music.

That's actually what makes musicians different from athletes. An athlete has to jump farthest and highest, run fastest. Their excellence is measurable. Music, on the other hand, is an art form. Let's say you buy a painting and hang it up on your wall. Five years later, you still enjoy looking at it. That means it must be good, right? But then someone else comes to visit and they don't like the painting at all. Music simply can't please everyone. You can't take a tape measure to determine if the music is good. When your listeners are happy, they think something like this: "Wow, that was great. I must go to this guy's next concert. What a great night. This was so relaxing." People don't just listen to the music; they need the complete experience. Experiences are extremely important for people today.

When you see all those stressed-out people running around, knowing they have 30 minutes to go down an elevator, grab a burger and fries, wash them down with a large Coke and then ride up again, you can practically see their ulcers growing. Life shouldn't be such a rat race. For people like that, the short moment during which they can feel music (if they are even able to feel it) is like an antidote to this: a great way to relax their mind, heart, and soul.

IMAGINE THAT YOU'RE PLAYING AT A CONCERT AND BOTH YOU AND YOUR AUDIENCE GET INTO A FLOW STATE. IN THAT MOMENT, THE BRAIN STARTS PRODUCING FOUR IMPORTANT HORMONES.

First comes endorphin, which makes sure that as long as you stay in flow, you can't feel any pain, and your listeners won't feel their fatigue, even if the concert is long. The second hormone produced is dopamine, which gives you the feeling of reward and joy once you've finished playing. You don't need other people for that, but those who listen to you will actually get the same feeling. The third hormone is serotonin. If your listeners enjoy your music, they give you a round of applause, and you feel their joy as if it were yours. It's a mutual exchange: to be happy, you need to make someone else happy.

The last substance produced by your brain and released into your bloodstream is oxytocin, the hormone of love and trust. Once your audience is completely attuned to you, and you to them, you feel their love and they feel yours. That's what will keep them coming to your concerts.

(I often tell athletes to make the audience start cheering for them before making that jump or throw. Feeling the spectators' support will help them release the four "happiness hormones.")

I view my music as a complex thing. I don't just want to play the violin but everything else that goes with it. I need an audience to play for, and people need to have a reason to come to my concerts. I've been a freelance musician all my life, which is very unusual. Most professional musicians like the security of playing in an orchestra or teaching music. Unlike them, I'm always motivated to create new things. If I ever stopped doing that, I would no longer be able to support myself through my music. Also, I simply can't do what a thousand other people are doing. It's just the way I am.

HOW DID YOUR DAUGHTER COME TO PLAY THE VIOLIN?

(JULIE SVĚCENÁ IS ALSO A SUCCESSFUL VIOLINIST.)

Julie started playing the violin from very early in her childhood, even earlier than I did – she was four-and-a-half years old. She saw me playing and wanted to do it just like her daddy. She was talented, of course. When she started music school, however, things were difficult for her. In the Czech Republic, everybody thought she was just capitalizing on her father's name. She had to face a lot of envy and resentment. She always had to be better than other children to prove herself. Thankfully, she's met some good people, too. At international contests, the jurors were often from other countries. At the age of 16, Julie won the Concertino Praga international radio violin concert. The contest was anonymous, and only one of the jurors was Czech. Julie won first place. After she graduated from the Prague Conservatory, I told her it would be best if she started out somewhere where her family and her heritage wouldn't matter as much as they did here – preferably abroad, where she could make a name for herself entirely on her own merit. Thanks to a friend of mine, American violin professor Stephen Shipps, we met Rodney Friend, one of the world's best violin teachers and former concertmaster of the New York Philharmonic Orchestra. Julie played for him before he went back to England, and he offered to tutor her – first he gave her private lessons, and then she went on to study at the Royal Academy of Music in London. She is currently finishing her doctorate degree there. She and Rodney have been collaborating very closely. He's helped her to prepare for large concerts and performances.

HAVE YOU EVER FELT LIKE SHE HAS STOPPED ENJOYING IT, THAT SHE MAY WANT TO QUIT AND START DOING SOMETHING ELSE?

She's always enjoyed playing the violin tremendously. She's been through some hard times, but it has never spoiled her love for music and the instrument. That's why she's so good today, I think. She's won one of the world's most important violin contests, which only proves how much she loves playing. She works extremely hard. It makes me so happy to see how musical she is and that people keep coming to her concerts and recitals over and over again. It's the most important thing you need to make it in this field.

I remember that when Julie was born, the first thing I noticed was how long her fingers were. "Wow, look at those fingers," I said, "I think she's going to be a great violinist." "Give that man a drink," the doctor said, "I think he's in shock."

YOUR OTHER DAUGHTER, MICHAELA, GRADUATED FROM THE SCHOOL OF ECONOMICS, AND SHE'S ALSO VERY SUCCESSFUL IN WHAT SHE DOES.

Before she went on maternity leave, she used to work for one of the world's largest consulting companies. How did that come about? Did you also help her to develop her talents?

My wife had a lot more influence over Michaela than I did. I've always traveled a lot, and my wife had to accompany our youngest daughter, Julie, to all her contests and concerts. My wife is a former pianist – she went to the same school as I did – and Michaela, our eldest, has always loved the piano, even though she decided on a different career path in the end. She went to a very prestigious high school, which helped her to get accepted to three different colleges. She chose the School of Economics, majoring in taxes and audit. As a student, she won an internship with the ministry of finance and was sent to Brussels to study the harmonization of various tax systems within the EU. Her final paper was rated as one of the best in her year. It helped her to get a job with PricewaterhouseCoopers. Later, she worked for a major gas company. She simply has a passion for economics, and she keeps abreast with the latest developments in her field. She's currently on maternity leave.

WHAT ABOUT MICHAELA AND MUSIC?

She likes playing the piano, but it's only a hobby for her. I like to say that she's the only one in our family with a normal job. We're all passionate about music; she merely likes it. I'm actually glad that she's different. It's good that she knows what she wants and that she's chosen her own path.

FOR YOU, PLAYING THE VIOLIN WAS A CHILDHOOD DREAM COME TRUE.

You had an immense talent that you've managed to turn into a lifelong profession. What do you think are the three most important things you need to make your dream come true?

If you want to become a professional violinist, you need to realize that it's going to be a lifelong commitment. It's not like professional sports where your career ends at the age of 35. You need to stay good even when you turn 50 or 60. You can stay professionally active well into your 70s, as long as you put in the effort. You need to decide quite early whether this is really the path you want to take. Once the violin becomes your world, you have to give it everything. Actually, "have to" are not the right words. Once you choose the violin, you are going to *want* to do it. If it's something that you enjoy and that gives you a sense of fulfillment, you'll give it your best.

The life of a solo musician requires strict discipline and self-denial. It's a life of hard work and creative effort. You have to keep yourself healthy. If your hands stop working because of inflamed tendons or strained nerves – and this happens very often – you're done. It's good to be aware of all that.

Playing an instrument all your life requires determination and motivation. If you enjoy what you do, it propels you forward at full throttle – it won't let you just amble along. You also need to keep your determination fresh and strong.

Music also requires diligence and discipline.

YOU'RE A PART OF SHOW BUSINESS LIKE ANY OTHER ARTIST, WHICH MEANS THAT, BESIDES BEING A FIRST-CLASS SOLO MUSICIAN, YOU ALSO HAVE TO BE ABLE TO SELL YOUR ART.

Exactly. It's something that many musicians who play in an orchestra never realize. They have their place in the world, a sense of security, which often means they don't feel the need to improve and develop. They don't work as hard, and they have almost no self-promotion skills. That's something I have to work on day after day. I have to keep improving and innovating – otherwise I would have no chance of making it as a soloist.

INTERVIEW WITH DAGMAR SVOBODOVÁ, MOTHER OF THREE SONS

(MOTHER OF THREE SONS: DAVID, OLYMPIC CHAMPION IN MODERN PENTATHLON; TOMÁŠ, SUCCESSFUL TRIATHLETE AND TEACHER; AND PAVEL, CEO OF THE COMPANY ADASTRA)

WHAT WAS YOUR PARENTING APPROACH TOWARD YOUR SONS? DID YOU TREAT EVERY ONE OF THEM DIFFERENTLY?

I firmly believe that school is not the only source of education; you can learn from anyone, anywhere, and at any age. I think it's important to try out as many things as possible to improve your manual skills, productivity, and dexterity.

I come from a large family with a wide range of professions and careers, so I have had many different role models and experienced various approaches. I soon realized that with a lot of time and patience, or with a good teacher, you can do practically anything. I set out to find an activity for each of my three children that they would enjoy as much as possible but that would also utilize some of their talents and might one day turn into a career.

With our firstborn, Pavel, I actually still believed that graduating from college and having lots of hobbies and aptitudes (including artistic skills), a gift for music (he tried playing the piano, guitar, drums, and even started his own band and recorded an album), and athletic abilities (he tried about ten different sports and had an immense talent for ball games) would help a child achieve success and fulfillment both in his career and his personal life. Having been born in September, Pavel was one of the oldest kids in his class. He was mostly used to the company of adults. He'd always enjoyed reading, and the bulk of his leisure activities took place outside of school. He found most of his classes dull and boring. Providing distraction and enjoyment for such a universally gifted child is extremely hard, and usually requires a lot of money. It also complicated his choice of college – he simply couldn't decide where to go. Specialists from the education counseling center were not of much help; they told us he could study practically anything. Finally, I managed to find the answer by asking the right questions. Compared to other people, Pavel had extremely well-developed spatial perception; such a talent would come in handy in such fields as architecture – or, as Pavel soon found out, computer programming. First, he studied on his own, reviewed computer games, and started creating his own databases. He actually managed to turn this into a source of income well before he graduated high school. This only proves that traditional education is not very reliable as far as teaching new, fast-developing disciplines is concerned.

With the twins, David and Tom, I didn't have as much time for experimenting and trying out different things as I'd had with Pavel. I had to oversee twice as much homework, there were two voices constantly arguing, and I had to try and find something they would both have in common. In the long run, playing sports was the only thing that met all the factors we needed. We tried out various sports (and immediately excluded field hockey because the boys wore glasses and practice was tedious and dull) – but the time spent with other children playing in our backyard seemed just as important to me as organized training sessions.

WHAT DID YOU HAVE TO DO TO DEVELOP YOUR CHILDREN'S TALENTS?

First of all, I had to keep my family healthy. I focused on prevention and attended various lectures to learn how best to do it. I insisted on cold baths and swimming lessons in the pool, I watched the boys' diet carefully, I gave them vitamin supplements, and took them to the countryside on weekends. A simple head cold could disrupt our entire schedule – suddenly I had to decide whether to stay at home with the sick twin and let the other one go to his practice alone or leave the sick one alone at home and take the other one wherever he needed to be. I had to buy sports gear and clothing and run the household. When the boys were little, their grandparents helped pick them up from school, but in fifth grade they started going to school and to their swimming training on their own. When they decided to switch schools, I was supportive as long as they promised they would always get to school on time.

WHAT DO YOU THINK MAKES DAVID DIFFERENT FROM HIS BROTHERS?

I like to say that he's always been "seven minutes more determined." Compared to other children, he always took his training sessions very seriously. He stopped swimming in his sophomore year in high school, transferred from a sports-oriented school to a regular one, and commuted across the entire city to his new sports club. Tom had only switched to triathlon after his sophomore year.

David had never minded having his picture taken – in fact, he was the only one who was willing to pose for the boys' first professional photo. Tom adamantly refused, and for a very long time, we had no pictures of him at all, so we kept our family guessing which of the boys was actually in the picture or told them that, since they were identical, it didn't matter which one of them it was.

David had always known he wanted to compete in the Olympics one day, even if he didn't talk about it. He was never much of a person for sharing his thoughts and ambitions, but he worked as hard as he could. He needed me to create a harmonious environment for him, and I trusted that he knew best what he wanted. As soon as he started doing pentathlon, I realized that everything else took a back seat. I had to ask his coach to check whether he really went straight home from training because he had a tendency to overdo it. I met the coach at a competition some months later, and he told me that I'd been right: David would stay longer after his training and sneak into the older boys' sessions.

WHEN DID DAVID DECIDE HE WANTED TO DO MODERN PENTATHLON?

He was 16 at the time.

WAS HE ALWAYS AN ATHLETIC CHILD?

Yes. We were a very active family, and we wanted the boys to try out many different sports. David was a fast learner and liked pretty much everything. He never destroyed any of his equipment, never scraped a knee. Tom, on the other hand, broke countless pairs of eyeglasses – not while playing sports, though. I kept forbidding them to fight with each other, but you can probably imagine what went on in their room behind closed doors.

David was always a very fast learner. He was also very photogenic and looked good while doing pretty much anything. He didn't mind posing for photos, either. His first swimming coach, back in elementary school, praised him for his perfect style and chose him to make a video demonstrating various swimming strokes.

WHAT WOULD YOU TELL THOSE PARENTS WHO CAN'T DECIDE WHICH TYPE OF SPORT WOULD BE BEST FOR THEIR CHILD? HOW CAN THEY HELP THEIR CHILD CHOOSE?

I recommend testing the child's motor skills and athletic abilities at the nearest sports field. You should talk to your child about what they like doing and watch them run and move. There are a lot of things anyone can try: jump rope, climbing rope, ball games, trampoline jumping, wall bars, horizontal bar – all of which you can do at home. Start with teaching your child a simple forward roll before you put them on the slope and force them to ski.

Teach your child to swim and ride a bike. Let them try sprint and endurance runs. Learn their preferences, their fears, and phobias. Do they prefer winter or summer sports? Do they simply like doing a particular sport for fun, or do they also need to compete and win? Do they only like a particular sport because they get to use cool equipment or wear nice jerseys? Do they want to do a sport because it's popular, or because one of their friends is doing it? Only after you determine all this can you decide on a sport based on your child's abilities and character. Some kids like playing soccer because they get to be with a bunch of friends; some prefer to practice gymnastic moves on their own.

Don't forget to consider whether you have sufficient funds for your child's training and whether you can fit the training into your family schedule. Find out whether there's a stadium or a sports field within an acceptable distance. Decide whether you're willing to be your child's driver, supplier, sponsor, and sparring partner. If you feel like what you're doing is a huge sacrifice, you will only make your child feel guilty. When you finally settle on a sport, get to know the child's coach and their plans and ambitions for your child.

I always wanted my boys to try out as many things as possible, as long as they felt safe doing them: cycling, cross-country and downhill skiing, swimming, ice skating... I wanted them to be well-rounded. At a certain point, I let them decide whether they wanted to try out more sports or whether to focus on improving those they'd already been doing.

The most important thing, however, is to make sure your child has fun playing the sport of their choice and that they see it as a way to improve. Don't pressure your children into doing something they don't enjoy. I think we have managed not to do that with our children.

[28] In the business world, this approach is known as *positive leadership*.

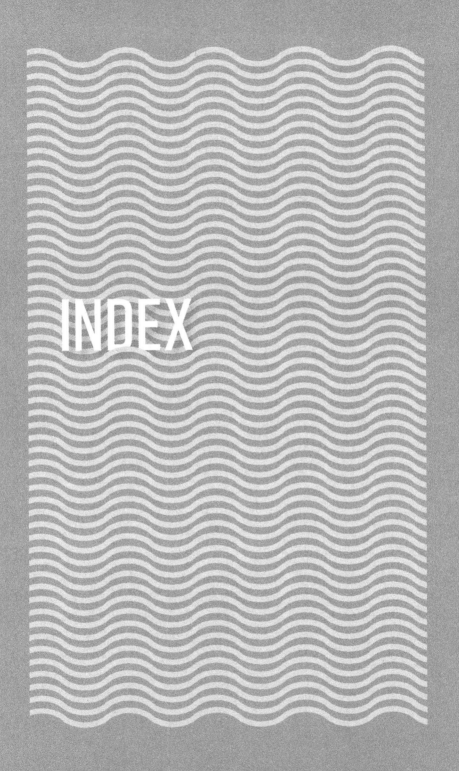

INDEX